**WHEREVER YOU ARE,
WHENEVER YOU DESIRE,
YOU CAN MAKE A
COMMITTED RELATIONSHIP
MORE EXCITING, MORE ALLURING,
AND HOTTER THAN EVER BEFORE...**

BEDROOM FUN AND GAMES

Discover the game of Blind Man's Bluff in which you guide your lover's mouth to your bared body, and then he or she must guess where he or she is kissing ... or the erotic "sculptor" and "painter" touching games.

AN "I LOVE YOU" DAY

Follow the step-by-step instructions for a morning-to-night special-loving day, with each event planned to deepen your bonds of intimacy, communicate your caring, and release your uninhibited desires.

GETAWAYS

Get travel plans for the most romantic vacations for couples, including a private island reserved just for lovers; an elegant, pampering train journey; or low-cost hideaways where lovers can focus on nothing but pleasuring each other.

St. Martin's Paperbacks Titles by Marie Papillon

A Million and One Love Strategies
Romancing the One You Love

Romancing the One You Love

Marie Papillon

St. Martin's Paperbacks

ROMANCING THE ONE YOU LOVE

Copyright © 1996 by Marie Papillon International, Inc.

ISBN: 0-312-95725-4

Printed in the United States of America

St. Martin's Paperbacks edition/February 1996

10 9 8 7 6 5 4 3 2 1

PREFACE

♥ ♥ ♥ ♥ ♥

There are so many nuances to the word *relationship*—from the first fragile, tenuous advances to the most profound, soul-searing involvement imaginable. Whatever temporary or permanent state a "relationship" is in at any given moment, fun and laughter are a shared bond, nourishing the growth and sweetening the depths of this primal need for companionship, acceptance, and love itself.

How can you encourage those moments of pure delight in each other's company? Keep alive the spark of spontaneity, the joy of shared laughter? The following tips and strategies will give you a rainbow of ideas: Your creativity can take it from there! Enjoy!

Romancing the
One You Love

Sensuous Pleasures

♥ ♥ ♥ ♥ ♥

Sensuality is the expression of your sexuality; it is a pleasuring of the senses, the luxuriating in the taste, smell, sound, touch, and sight of each other. Lovers who want to maximize those pleasurable sensations which they already enjoy when in each other's company, will delight in sampling this smorgasbord of delightful ideas for sensual enrichment.

The sense of touch is one of the most enduring of our memories of being loved, from childhood to adult relationships.

Because touching is so intricately involved with a feeling of being loved, whether holding hands, hugging, kissing, or exchanging intimate caresses, it is the one sense where a subtle introduction of an unexplored technique has remarkable impact.

For example, imagine you are sitting in a movie theater, or just chatting with friends and someone you love takes your hand and, instead of merely holding it, strokes each finger slowly and lovingly as though memorizing its texture. Is the immediate feeling one of being loved more deeply? Of a stronger bond of intimacy?

Now think of taking that simple gesture to a full-body massage with warm, scented oils. Your eyes have suddenly grown bigger and brighter and you are smiling! That's your sensuality at work—touching your mind with suggestion even before you touch the one you love.

Learn how to give a massage by taking a lesson or two or by reading books or watching instructional videos.

A good massage is far more than just running your hands over a bared body. For a relaxing massage, use warm, scented oils as you gently knead the shoulders, upper arms, thighs, and calves. By all means learn to give a great foot rub— including pulling each toe slightly and massaging the toe joints. This type of massage feels so great it will keep the love of your life at your feet—metaphorically speaking!

There are all types of massages—from therapeutic to relaxing to erotic. Study them all and practice on each other. You will feel better in more ways than one!

Try mashed fruits and/or vegetables in place of massage oils.

At the Oriental Hotel in Bangkok, the masseuse uses mashed fresh papaya. Try your favorite tropical fruit—banana, mango, or pineapple. Add a dash of lemon or orange juice for a tingly effect.

To add a second sensual note to the massage, have music playing softly in the background. New Age, classical, or the sounds of birds, beaches, and water for relaxation; Oriental, Hawaiian, or island rhythms for a more exotic atmosphere.

For a more playful "touching" experience, play "sculptor."

You can really get into the spirit of this activity by dressing the part. A big see-through shirt and beret for a woman sculptor and brief black briefs and a beret for a man. What does the person whose body is to be sculpted wear? What any sensible statue wears, of course—*nothing!*

Whether you are sculpting an ice block, a cake of soap, or a lump of clay—or just pantomiming—the sculptor must, of course, touch the sculptee *a lot!* To get a "feel" for the subject, naturally!

A variation on the above theme is "the Perfectionist Tailor."

In this "touching" scenario, both participants may start off fully clothed, but as the "fitting" progresses, various articles may be dispensed with. When measuring the arms, for example, how can you have anything covering them? And measuring around the chest must be done at nipple level. Slide the tape around a bit here. Measuring the wrists can also be entertaining if you insist on the hands being placed on the (bare) chest of the one doing the measuring. Getting the tape in the proper position around the posterior can be a fun maneuver, as is getting the all-important "inseam" measurement correct. This particular "number" may need to be reassessed several times!

Developing your talent as a "weekend painter" may become a regular activity when you practice your "art" on each other.

Using easily washable waterbased paints, decorate the body of your love, slowly and artistically, with your fingers. Take turns painting each other. Even more fun by candlelight! Or go for a glow-in-the-dark mural using fluorescent paint sticks! Do you dare take color Polaroid pictures?

It is not recommended that you try this activity on a sleeping partner. Ben was nearly finished painting a glorious sunflower on Betty when she awakened. It took three shampoos to get all the orange paint out of his blond hair!

The surface you lie upon can be the basis for a deeply sensual experience.

Everyone has experienced the simple pleasure of getting into a freshly made bed with the linens lightly scented from the wash or a favorite perfume. Some have likened this delight for the senses to lying down in a meadow. Can you imagine the terrific feeling of actually lying on soft flower petals?

Lorraine decided to surprise Ken in this way. She bought dozens of wide-open fragrant roses and a small bottle of rose-scented perfume. She placed lighted candles (also rose-scented) about the room and set out a vase of some of the flowers. She separated the rest of the roses and spread the rose petals on the pale pink percale bottom sheet. She scented the rose-printed pillowcases with the perfume and put on a pale rose-colored gown. When Ken entered the room a few moments later, he was pleasantly surprised by the colors and scents and enchanted with the idea of sleeping on flower petals.

The two of them have never forgotten the wonderful feel of the satiny soft rose petals and the delicate scent they left on their skin . . . and the love they shared on a bed of roses!

Experiment with the "feel" of your bedding.

Spread baby power or lightly scented body or talcum powder on bedsheets. Your skin will feel amazingly soft and the sheets will give the sensation of sleeping on soft, fluffy clouds!

Buy a set of luxurious, sensually glorious satin sheets and pillowcases. You'll love the slip-slip-slidin' around—and no body burns!

If you adore the sensations of making love on a waterbed but your loved one doesn't like one for sleeping on, buy a waterbed for the guest bedroom and slip in there when the two of you want to "make waves!"

Touching also involves the little gestures that establish intimacy and delight in each other.

Hugs of all types—from the quick "Hello!" to the full "bear" hug are delightful demonstrations of the desire to be close to the object of our affections. There are also numerous other minicaresses that are highly effective. A pat on the back, an arm around a shoulder, a surreptitious grab at an irresistible derriere—all say "I want to be near to you, you are attractive to me, you are important to me." Touch is a great communicator: Don't leave home without it!

The mouth is undoubtedly one of the more sense intensive organs of the body, incorporating taste and touch. And the lips rival the hands in administering the tenderest and most erotic range of expressive touching.

Although Jerome Kern's famous song claims that a kiss is only a kiss, truly sensuous kissing doesn't stop at serious pressing of two mouths together! Try kissing the corners of your love's mouth, sucking and biting a bit. Use the same technique on their nipples. Yes, *men* have sensitive nipples, too! Gently kiss and nip erogenous zones—like the back of the knee, the back of the neck, the entire backbone, the arch of the foot, the earlobes, the top of the shoulder, that diabolical spot just above the elbow. Drift a fingertip up and down a bared torso and follow that trail with a flutter of kisses. Powerful!

What more fun could there be for both of you than in perfecting the Venus Butterfly, that classic, passion-soaring mouth-to-love's-lips favorite of erotic literature!

Sensuous, romantic kissing is not necessarily heavily passionate.

In the famous scene in the movie, *Age of Innocence,* when the lover, actor Daniel Day-Lewis, slowly unbuttons and removes the glove of the heroine, actress Michelle Pfeiffer, kisses her wrist and then the palm of her hand, the romantic tension between them practically shoots fireworks off the screen! This simple action can be carried out in full daylight—even by candlelight—in public places like a restaurant. Inherent in the eroticism of this gesture in full view of others is that this overture of love must wait for its finale until the couple are alone!

Play a combination of Blind Man's Bluff and a Name That Place kissing game.

Blindfold your darling, gently tie their hands together behind their back, and then guide their mouth to a spot on your bared body. Using only a kiss, they have to tell you *where* they are kissing. Does an upper arm feel the same to the lips as a lower arm? Is the hollow in your elbow similar to the hollow behind your knee? Kiss and Tell Geography is a fun game. Score one point for each correct guess. Five points and then it's your turn to wear the blindfold!

Sensuous touching is not confined to the mouth and hands.

Try this "dance of love" to warm up a cold (k)night. Start off by slow-dancing to your favorite music or throbbing rhythms. As your bodies touch, begin removing a piece of clothing each, one piece at a time. His shirt, her blouse; his trousers, her slacks or skirt. His socks, her stockings. Try dancing back to back, touching shoulderblades and underwear-clad bottoms. Switch to front to front. See how long you can go on teasing each other by touching bared bodies only—no lips or hands. Until you finally reach a point where this is *it!* It will be fantastic!

Let your sense of touch help you to truly "learn" your love's body.

Everyone's body has firm and soft areas, sensitive ticklish ones, and those that need a firmer touch or pressure to respond. What is the texture of your love's body hair? The hair on their head? Explore each other with fingertips, toes, lips, back of the hand. Your "lessons of each other" will lead to a renewed closeness and a sense of the richness and diversity of your love's body map.

Here's a kissable idea guaranteed to "light up the night!"

Map your erogenous zones with tiny glow-in-the-dark hearts. Turn out the lights and invite your partner to track your pathway of love with kisses. That circlet of hearts around your ankle is really inventive—and delightful! This game gives a whole new meaning to the "Glow Little Glow Worm" lyrics!

Taste sensations are libido raisers—particularly when you combine the heady rush of sweet chocolate with a lickin' good body!

Your love will never be able to look at chocolate sauce again without getting a "love rush" when you try this erotic combo! Spread chocolate fudge sauce or Nutella on various parts of your anatomy. A dab in the little hollow in your throat, your belly button depression. Slather some on your nipples and other erogenous zones, like behind your knees.

Your significant other won't need a gold-edged invitation to this feast! Does chocolate give him or her hives? Use whipping cream—or maple syrup!

For a really fantastic weekend dessert, try Sunday Sundaes.

This positively splendid high-calorie love treat is the super-pluperfect sundae or banana split—on you! Literally! Start with a generous dollop of chocolate fudge or caramel sauce. Add a few squirts of whipped cream, and top with banana slices and a cherry. Try not to laugh: The whole concoction will slide off your tummy before your sweetie gets a bite.

If you are the one invited to this love feast, say you think the ice cream is missing and cool your tongue in a glass of ice water before you begin tummy-licking. Serves them right!

This fun little exercise can get a bit messy. If using a bed, cover with old linens. But aren't desserts usually served on the dining room table? Or in the living room? *Draw those drapes, puhleeze!!!*

Perhaps the most evocative of the sensual pleasures is the power of scent.

You have no doubt heard of the effects of scent on the libido. In addition to the natural human pheromones which make you feel relaxed and friendly, there are the manufactured scents that have the ability to call up memories of pleasurable activities. Vanilla is often associated with the anticipation of childhood sweets, as is an undernote of cinnamon. Light citrusy/woodsy/flowery accents represent innocence and freshness, while the heavier, opulent Oriental/tropical-flowered, sandalwood/musk-note perfumes are provocatively seductive.

You can either elect to have one personal fragrance "signature" that reflects your personality, or have a range of scents—compatible with your skin's chemistry—that enhance your mood or a setting you wish to evoke. Either way, your choice should be designed to work the desired magic on your significant other!

Once you have chosen a fragrance, make it an integral part of your surroundings.

Use touches of your "signature" scent to mark your surroundings. Put sachets in bureau drawers or in pillowcases and choose candles that release one of the "notes" in your special fragrance. Saturate cotton balls with your choice of perfume or cologne and place one in your car, your briefcase, your purse. Slip one into his luggage: He will be reminded of you throughout the trip. Use a dab on stationery when penning even a casual note. Just keep in mind that a perfume should be discernible enough to remind him of you, but not so strong it can walk into an elevator unaided!

It is stimulating to vary the fragrances you use in the bedroom and throughout the house.

The scent of pine can recall that wonderful time the two of you made love deep in a quiet forest. Or a light spritz of a spray that smells of the sea can transport you to that idyllic night under the stars at a Caribbean resort.

Fresh, lemon-scented candles can be a lovely accompaniment to dinner, and the exotic fragrance of ginger or cinnamon stimulates conversation and erotic thoughts!

The sound of a loved one's voice is a powerful libido stimulant.

Why should you leave messages on your love's answering machine? Why should you make an effort to talk to them several times during the day? Why should you strive to keep your voice pleasing in tone? Because your voice stirs deep sensations of pleasure, desire, and a longing to see you.

It is more the sound of your voice than the words you are actually saying that evokes this need to be with you. Strive for a loving, caring tone with subtle undernotes of sexual desire. It is so very easy to slip into a bored, casually offhand manner of speaking by phone if you do not concentrate on the person with whom you are talking. A strong mental image will have to do until VideoVision phones are more affordable and more widely available!

Music is, of course, one of the master communicators of feelings. For background loving, your best bet is instrumental.

When you look back over the most compelling love sequences you have experienced, very often you recall that music was playing in the background—real or imaginary. Perhaps this is due to our movie-oriented courtship training, or the fact that so many daily activities are underscored by musical sounds. For most people, there are specific songs that have deep emotional ties, and hearing these songs releases a virtual flood of memories and associated feelings. This can be a plus in most situations, but when "there's a whole lot of lovin' goin' on," music without vocals is preferable so that you can concentrate on the words and sounds of passion you and the one you love are exchanging, not an anonymous, disembodied voice telling you what you should be feeling—or doing!

Decide on pet phrases to indicate to each other that you are aroused—or want to be!

Suppose you are at a party and you realize you would rather be enjoying the one you love—alone! When you have a pre-arranged signal or phrase prepared, you can get your message across without revealing anything to others. Of course you will need to choose something innocuous, like "Isn't this a terrific evening for walking the dog?" or "I thought I smelled something burning." On the way home, raise the heat between you by telling, in great detail, just what you have in mind to do. Who can blame your loved one for dropping the house keys and accidentally setting off the alarm?

Gently tell your loved one what you want from him or her and how you are responding to his or her loving technique.

There are few sounds more likely to arouse a lover than the murmurs and sighs of appreciation for his or her efforts. Take these indications a step further by being precise about what you need from your lover to heighten your experience. Lovers want to please each other, and how is another person to know what movements, caresses, words, or techniques fuel your mutual ecstasy engine if you don't explain? The only time terrific lovemaking requires the silent treatment is if you have stopped an elevator between floors for a love nest!—or similar fun/dangerous/*Shhhhh!* location!

Using a low, sultry voice, read erotic poetry or passages from erotic books to your "teddy bear."

There are many erotically charged books with long descriptive passages of lovemaking or love encounters. Try those written by Anais Nin or Henry Miller, for example. There is a journal called *Yellow Silk* that features erotic poetry and essays. Even reading love poems by Byron, Shelley, Browning, Keats, or one of the modern poets will lend a special air of love and magic to your "pillow talk." Set the scene—a virtual garden of sensual delights—with lowered lights, bouquets of flowers, scented candles, soft music, satin pillows, and your romantic self!

Tired of routine beddy-byes? Rent sexy videos or tune in to an X-rated movie channel.

Bring the small screen to big life by imitating the sexual antics on adult videos or on an uncensored movie channel. Set limits that you are both comfortable with: no rough stuff, no bondage, nothing masochistic, for example. This is supposed to be *loving!*

The sense of sight is a powerful aphrodisiac.

The sight of a loved one incites the deepest feelings of tenderness, caring, and desire. The eyes brighten, the pupils dilate, the mouth becomes fuller, the skin becomes more sensitized, the heart beats faster, and lovers even may experience spasms of delight just from looking at each other. The same idea holds true in intimate lovemaking. By looking directly at your lover's eyes, smiling into them, letting them see the love and pleasure in your face and in your eyes, the total loving experience will be enhanced. Dare to experience heightened arousal: Open your eyes!

Setting the stage for lovemaking is a caring, intensely romantic gesture.

In the early stages of a relationship, the bright newness of love and its pure physical intensity may leave any interest in surroundings relegated to no more than a casual observation. Dishevelled beds are fond reminders of the ecstasy, unkempt rooms of the disorder of love. But there comes a point when either of the couple begins to take pride in setting the stage, in taking care that their surroundings are a reflection and an inspiration of love.

It is at this point that the beautiful bed linens and soft cushions, the drifts of tulle draped from hooks in the ceiling above the bed, the carefully arranged mirrors, lamps, candles, books, rugs, and other items reflect a desire for an outward air of romance to sweeten and deepen the experience of romantic encounters.

A nicely appointed room is a delight to both the eye and the heart, and a person who takes the time and makes the effort to create a warmly welcoming ambience will be rewarded with appreciative loving. Flowers, scented candles, clean, freshly laundered bed linens, and soft lighting and music *do* make a difference! Why not add a bedside box of luscious, aphrodisiacal chocolate delights—in sexy shapes, perhaps?—to your shopping list?!

Excite all your love's senses with a stimulating guessing game.

While Eric was drying off after his pre-bedtime shower, Marnie slipped a blindfold over his eyes, led him into the bedroom and sat him on the bed. She had prepared a Test Your Senses game with a range of things for him to taste, feel, smell, and hear. She promised to remove the blindfold *after* he "passed" the "test." Using a seductive voice and light caresses, Marnie put a dab of peanut butter in the cleavage between her breasts and guided Eric's mouth to it. He identified the peanut butter, but needed some prompting to discover where it was placed.

Next, Marnie slipped a silky satin robe over her curvaceous body. She sat on Eric's lap and asked him to run his hands over her and identify the type of material she was wearing. She knew the feel of satin was a turn-on for Eric, and enjoyed his groan of pleasure and his exploration of the sensuous material.

Then Marnie held various vials of essential oils near Eric's nose, being sure to include the most aphrodisiacal—rose, jasmine, cinnamon, clove, and gardenia—all of which he was able to identify. She dabbed her personal perfume—White Shoulders—on her wrist and asked him to identify the scent. He did, and surprised Marnie by kissing her long and passionately! Obviously all his senses were aroused—but his sight! Eric was finally permitted to remove the blindfold—*after* they had lovingly satisfied each other!

Act out a sensuous scene from a sexy movie.

An all-star cast of you and your love can make a reenactment of a seduction scene a four-star success! Choose something you both would like—perhaps from *Dirty Dancing, Pretty Woman, Sleepless in Seattle, When Harry Met Sally, The Piano, The Lover*—even a scene from an old foreign film that you found particularly arousing. If you can't remember all the words, improvise. It's the sexual tension and interaction that you are aiming for. If you can't decide on a scene, invent one! Take your time. Do all the slow, romantically charged preludes to love that you can imagine, such as taking your love's face in your hands and gazing lovingly into his or her eyes. Follow up by slowly undressing your love and kissing his or her body as it is revealed. What a great way to build up sexual tension! Would you dare videotape *your* steamy seduction scene?

Is your lovelife so steamy it would fog up a mirror? Put it to the test!

This major love booster takes a little planning, but the results should be worth it. Buy a large mirror and install it on the ceiling above your bed. *Make certain the mirror is securely attached.* Stick hearts and cupids on it if you wish. *Do not tell your special person about this ahead of time.* Keep the lighting level low—lots of candlelight preferred—and the music soft and sweet. You will know when they have spotted the ceiling "mural" by the sharp intake of breath and a little scream of disbelief. When the shock wears off, enjoy your new "movie screen!"

Role-playing scenarios can get you "in the mood."

Play-acting can be a lot of fun and a real turn-on when you use a combination of visual and verbal clues. Try playing Boss and Private Secretary—with a modern twist: the *female* is the boss who dictates letters brimming with innuendoes while a scantily clad *Mr.* P. S. sits on her lap.

Or try the old favorite of the milkman or mailman and the housewife who insists on "special delivery."

For a spicier scenario, try these "snaps."

It's also stimulating for some couples to play *Playboy* photographer and centerfold model. All that posing—and all those famous positions—can be very erotic. Switch roles and do a Chippendales calendar! Music with a definite beat is a stimulating background!

Fulfilling your love's sexual fantasies is a very intimate, ultimately caring gift of yourself.

If your lover's fantasies are not so far out that you could be comfortable participating, surprise him or her by offering to fulfill his or her deepest wants. Having shared these most intimate thoughts with you has demonstrated trust and by expressing your desire to respond, you are giving your lover what is perhaps the ultimate gift a loving couple can offer each other.

For example, does your love's dream desire for hot sex in the washroom of a fast-moving train suggest a longing for more excitement during your lovemaking? You could take that need and translate it into something you *are* willing to do, such as seducing him or her during a walk in the woods, or making love in the living room around the time guests are to arrive!

Should the man in your life say he fantasizes being made love to by two or three women at a time, raise your attention level two or three degrees—show and tell him how irresistible you find him. Or have him close his eyes and describe what each of the women is doing to him at the same time. That, too? *Wow!*

With love and imagination, the two of you can fulfill each other's deepest sexual needs and desires—but only in those instances where the fantasy does not mean inflicting humiliation or pain on either of you.

Really? You're going for a walk in the woods wearing just your trench coats? Again?

Keep your pre-lovetime conversations centered around pleasurable topics.

Even if you haven't planned on a particularly sensuous evening, keep pre-bedtime talkfests light and filled with pleasant memories or of anticipated pleasures—like the upcoming musical you plan to attend. The fastest way to dampen a "mood" is to start making lists—verbal or written—of jobs that need doing or that you want your significant other to do. Going over the budget, the children's problems at school, talking about bills, complaining about anything from the dog needing a bath to how Aunt Celia neglects to call before she visits—all of these are no-no topics whether you want maximum love attention or a restful night's sleep. Mentioning how much you like that silk bathrobe and how the color makes her skin glow, or telling him how you got that intense interior thrill of pleasure when he walked in the door, *that's* bedtime conversation!

Make a point of preparing yourselves mentally and physically for an evening of loving.

Fabulous lovemaking is often a culmination of a number of small acts and loving thoughts over a period of time. A lingering kiss in the morning, a telephone call during the day just to say hello, a card, a poem, a few flowers, a specialty chocolate, just a few compliments or words of appreciation and thanks, a caring gesture or caress, something as simple as helping with the dishes—even a silly, inexpensive gift, makes the recipient feel special, cared for, and open to more intimate expressions of love.

Now that you've got your love there, do something different or frivolous—or both!

When you and your lover have slipped between the sheets, whisper something suggestive like, "You really tickle my fancy!" And do it! Tickling each other is childish, but great fun—to a degree! Turned on—not gasping for breath—is the goal!

Do you dare try this at his/her office?

If your lover has a *very* private office, you might want to surprise him or her with a visit from a personal masseuse: you!

Use a sports bag to carry an assortment of scented massage oils, big fluffy towels, a roll-up mat, candles, a tape of soft, relaxing music—perhaps some sandalwood incense to heighten the mood. It's guaranteed to be an experience he or she won't forget!

Penetrate the confines of his/her office with a sensual "Love Box."

Prepare a "Love Box" to send to your darling's office. Include such items as exotic bath oils, cologne, fluffy towels, a luxurious bathrobe and a small bottle of champagne. Wrap the box beautifully and decorate with a big red bow. Enclose a note with as detailed instructions as you like, telling the lucky person what you have planned for your "bathing date" that evening. Count on their being home early!

Couples need to discuss the realization that there are different types of sexual encounters, and there is no need to conform to a particular norm.

In the course of any relationship there will be a wide range of intimate expressions of love—everything from a "quickie" lasting for a few minutes to a love marathon that can go on for hours. When a couple can discuss openly the fact that all of these moments of lovemaking are basically and sincerely a display of love, neither partner will feel pressured to perform to the max. In other words, striving to achieve a ten on an imaginary orgasmic scale is not necessary *every* time.

Have special code words that not only signal that you are ready for an intimate encounter, but what kind.

When couples are pressured for time but want and need an intimate moment, it is easier to ask in such a way that both partners know what parameters to expect. Having special "love words" that tell your darling you want and need "the big one" or just a comforting cuddle goes a long way toward keeping your relationship buzzing with happiness.

Stuck in traffic with your loved one? Make the most of these moments together.

Here you are, the two of you, caught in a traffic jam. Prepare for just such little emergencies by keeping an erotic novel, a cassette tape of the sexiest songs you can find, a battery-operated body vibrator, and a small vial of exotic body massage oil in the glove compartment. Use your imagination. Traffic tie-ups will never be boring timewasters again!

Reserve at least one dresser drawer for sexy nightwear — and use it!

Feeling in the mood and want to show it? Now is *not* the time to rummage through drawers and closets for that sexy black teddy or see-through negligee you got for Christmas. Keeping your play clothes ready for action makes it easier to "seize the moment." Let him know where you keep your "lovin' duds" and he might surprise you by handing you that black lace number instead of a towel when you're stepping out of the shower!

Store "love toys" in a special, locked treasure chest and give him one of the keys to carry in his wallet.

Keep a supply of unusual condoms, ultra-sexy underwear, massage oils, and any other creams, gels, or "toys" you use for your most intimate moments in a special "treasure chest." Keep it locked and give your darling one of the keys to carry in a place where he will see it often and be reminded of your shared passion. Make sure you have an extra key stashed in your bedroom—in case he left his wallet at the office!

You can also use the key as a signal to each other that loving is on your mind. Press your key into his hand when he comes home from work and watch his eyes light up. Imagine the anticipation that builds as the evening goes on, dinner is over, and the kids are finally in bed! Isn't that a rather *large* treasure chest???

Plan a mini treasure hunt—with a delightful difference!

This treasure hunt is particularly effective if you have to be out for an evening and your darling is home alone. Leave a note taped to the fridge that instructs him to look in the freezer for a further clue. On a chilled, chocolate heart, tape a note that directs him to the cabinet where you keep the wine glasses. Have another note that leads to a small bottle of red wine or a soft drink you both like. The next note tells him that he is getting warmer and sends him to the bathroom where you have everything ready for a bubblebath for two. A note on the bathroom mirror says there is a special delight waiting in the bedroom. Have a sexy nightie and silk briefs spread out on the bed. Don't be surprised if you are greeted at the door with Mr. Silk Shorts handing you the nightie— or vice versa!

Is your darling's passion chocolate chip cookies? Treat his taste buds with this titillating scenario.

Larry loved chocolate chip cookies—even the uncooked dough! One evening he came home from work to find his petite wife wearing a chocolate-chip-cookie-dough bikini. She didn't have to ask him twice if he wanted a bite!

To keep your lovelife XXX-rated, keep your darling guessing!

Georgie learned that her husband, Wayne, was tripping off to a local strip joint regularly. Instead of creating a scene, she decided to become his favorite "tease." One week she pretended she was the "madam" in charge of a group of "naughty girls" and proceeded to play all the roles—a different one each night.

Another time she swathed herself in layers of scarves and removed them slowly in time to provocative music. Wayne was so intrigued with not knowing what "person" he would discover next that he abandoned the strip joint for his "home entertainment center."

Keep adding new items to your "intimate moments" collection.

Variety is the spice of life—and doubly so in the bedroom. Invest in sexy items like a red satin G-string, flavored condoms, edible undies, and fun items like glow-in-the-dark body paint or tassel-twirling pasties. Look for items that let you be seductive, irresistible, spontaneous. Give yourself the pleasure of a lighthearted, fun approach to lovemaking and you'll be surprised at how sexy it makes *both* of you feel!

Play into a range of fantasies by acting "good" and "bad."

Just for the fun of it, call your lover at work and, in a sweet, innocent voice, say you have heard what a terrific, gentle lover he is and that he is the one you want for your "first time." Keep the fantasy going when he arrives home by dressing all in white—with a high collar and long sleeves, if possible. Pretend to be demure and shy. Let him "persuade" you.

Another time, call and tell him you have been given his number by a friend as *the one* to contact for a "hot" time. Be as explicit as you dare. Now is the time to wear that sexy number with the low back and the cleavage-city front! Slip on a pair of high heels and add sexy-spicy perfume and low lights—candlelight perhaps? Flirt outrageously and enjoy your "act!"

Trying too hard to be "the sexiest thing on two feet" can have the opposite effect.

Religiously following "experts'" instructions on positions and techniques can get the two of you so involved in concentrating on the "how" that you lose the "why"—your feelings. True sensuality is based on your acceptance of what pleases you and being comfortable enough with your partner to let him or her know what you are experiencing physically and emotionally. Using words like "there," "now," and "*mmmmnnnn* good!" are a good beginning.

FUN REASONS FOR MAKING LOVE—NOW

It's raining.
It's snowing.
It's the longest night of the year.
It's the shortest night of the year.
There's a full moon.
There's a "blue" moon.

There's a new moon.
There's an eclipse.
You saw a falling star and made this your wish.
You have tickets to a fireworks exhibition and want to set
     the mood.
Your horoscope said tonight is the night.
The beach looks soft and inviting in the moonlight.
You rented a yacht for the evening.
You need inspiring.
You are inspired.
Your arms are aching—to hug your loved one.
Your nose is itchy.
You need to practice your flute fingering—on a body.
Your mother-in-law just left.
Your phone is out of order.
The vet says your guppy is pregnant.
You just feel sexy!
You want to express your love.
You need some distraction.
You just took a lovely bubble bath.
You want to try out your new cologne.
You just lit a hundred candles and the light is so romantic.
You rented a sexy video and want to act it out.

You just became an aunt/uncle.

You just got a promotion.

You just lost your job.

You did not get a promotion.

Your boss doesn't know you're back from your business trip.

You test drove a Rolls-Royce and don't want to waste the thrill.

You just put a bottle of Moet & Chandon champagne on ice

You promise to go out and buy champagne—for breakfast.

You just ate half a pound of Godiva chocolates—and you know what they say about chocolates and aphrodisiacs.

You are starting a new diet tomorrow.

You're wearing a new nightgown/pajamas/lingerie.

You're itching to get out of your scratchy new flannel nightgown/pajamas.

You're feeling great/happy/excited/really "up"!

Your new motto is: "Carpe Diem—Seize the Moment!"

Your partner looks just so great/terrific/wonderful/unforgettable.

The national norm is ten times a month and you're down
  five.
You have the afternoon off.
There's nothing worth watching on TV.
Today has been a great day.
Tomorrow is another day.
It's the first nice day of the week.

***"Kidnapped" weekends are a popular way to add
excitement and private time to a relationship.***

The location for a "mystery" weekend can be as simple as a
few days at a charming inn nearby to a faraway, exotic island.
The main element is anticipation—laced with a healthy dose
of surprise.

Ellen called Don on Wednesday and told him she would pick
him up when he finished work on Friday, and not to plan
anything for the weekend. She did not tell him she had made
reservations at a local spa for a day of pampering on Saturday
as well as dinner and room reservations at a neighboring ho-

tel. The glow of this terrific time together brought smiles to their faces for weeks afterward!

Today, Don called Ellen and told her to pack a suitcase of casual clothes. *You* finish the scenario!

How can you manage to add miniholidays to a budget?

Many couples would dearly love to take a minivacation, but do not see any way possible to find the extra money to do so. Because getting away together—alone!—is so often crucial to reestablishing the closeness of the early days of being together, a couple may want to try one or more of the following suggestions:

♥ Put a dollar in a special get-away-from-it-all box every time you make love.

♥ Deposit ten to twenty dollars in a special savings account every time you go to the bank. Also, if another bank pays higher interest, move your account.

* Have a garage sale and get rid of all those items you don't need and don't want—but *somebody* does.

* Take a good hard look at any investments or insurances you have and see if the funds can be moved into higher earning financial vehicles.

* Look for an odd job or a service you could provide one day or evening a week and put that money into your special fund.

* Whenever you use grocery coupons, put the money saved into your getaway fund.

* Save on dry-cleaning bills by washing woolen sweaters and skirts in cold water and Woolite or Zero. Put the estimated savings in your special fund.

* Look for ways to save on electricity—like turning the thermostat down on your hot water heater, and shutting it off altogether when you go away for a few days. Your electricity company may even have booklets with tips on saving.

♥ Rejuvenate your wardrobe with inexpensive accessories and look for shops that have high-quality, classic secondhand clothing.

♥ Buy paper goods and detergents in bulk and slip the savings into your "love" fund.

♥ Decide to save one or two denominations of coins and stash them religiously in your fund.

♥ If possible, take a packed lunch to work.

♥ Look for ways to save on entertainment, like going to movie matinees instead of evenings, or having everybody contribute to "potluck" dinners when you entertain good friends.

As you can see, there are any number of "loopholes" in managing family finances that can result in a considerable amount of money saved in a relatively short time. And try your luck at entering all the contests that offer free trips for two—*somebody* wins them and it might just be the two of you!

*Keep your relationship energy high with spontaneous fun/
sexy actions.*

Do you have a spare bedroom, attic, or storage room that
locks? Why not wrap the key in ribbons and put it in a sealed
envelope along with instructions to meet you there at a certain time? Meanwhile, you have made the room into a love
bower with fancy bed linens, scented candles, flowers, music,
and sexy you!

Wrap up a fun scenario! Layers and layers of silks, laces, and
satins, starting with a fancy garter belt and brassiere, adding
a silk nightie, then a negligee, all topped with a floor-length
terry bathrobe—or a fur coat! A man could start with sexy
briefs topped with silk boxer shorts, pajamas, a robe, and a
trench coat.

This "bundling" more or less forces your partner to undress
you—or for you to perform an exotic striptease!

An added touch: As each piece of clothing is removed, say
what you are going to do once you are completely free of
these "bonds!" Help is on the way—fast!

Give your lovemaking a touch of adventure tinged with the possibility of discovery

Have you ever tried making love in the car when it's parked in your garage? Or in the laundry room? What about late at night under the bushes in the backyard? The children's tree house? A number of couples have found a love haven behind a locked bathroom door, and some adventurous souls have taken off more than their coats in the hall closet!

There is even a special club for those who have dared to make maximum use of "the facilities" on airplanes to engineer lovemaking in very tight quarters!

If money is no problem, hire a luxurious private plane and soar to new heights making love among the clouds!

Discover what is really important to the one you love.

It is so very easy to misread and misunderstand each other in a close relationship. Each of us has our own filter of experiences through which all words and gestures of those dearest to us are comprehended. If lovers are to know one another on many levels, they need to understand what things truly matter to their partner.

One lighthearted way to discover more about each other is to pose the question, "If you only had one more day—or week, or month—to live, what would you want to do? What would be the focus of those remaining hours or days?"

Although this philosophical question is posed in somewhat the same vein as the lighter ones of "What books, records and three personal items would you take with you if you were to be stuck on an island alone for three months? For a lifetime?" the question is meant to reveal those things which are of profound interest and worthy of concentrated mental and physical energy. It might be wise to check whether a prospective lover's response is compatible with yours *before* becoming romantically involved.

Sharing your inner thoughts is as important as sharing your dreams and fantasies—or your opinions!

When you first wake up in the morning, are you glad to see the one you love beside you? Don't just think it, *tell him— or her—so!* During the day, are you suddenly overcome with a strong wave of sexual desire for your mate? Pick up the phone and tell him—in suggestive detail. He might be inspired to suggest a picnic—in bed! Even if he can't rush to your side, you'll both be smiling for a while!

Little actions can spell big romance—and it's easy to fit these loving-energy suggestions into your day.

Finding time to be romantic is not as difficult as it may seem. How much time does it take to do the following "loving gestures" that add up to a *big* measure of romance?

▼ A hug and a kiss—even a lop-sided sitting-down one.

▼ Blow a kiss and mouth "I love you!" when your partner is on the phone or watching TV, or cooking or cleaning or doing some other chore.

♥ Grab your partner for a few minutes of really close slow-dancing when your favorite music is playing.

♥ Add candlelight and music to a regular dinner at home—and dress up as though you were going out.

♥ Try a minicompliment—like "You smell so nice!" or "Have I told you lately that you have beautiful eyes?"

♥ Slip an appointment card into your lover's agenda for him or her to fill in the date, time, dress code, and *place*—for a lovemaking session.

Look for little ways to regain and to redevelop a friendship with your mate.

Many couples begin their relationship as friends and then unconsciously drift toward a position of benign neglect or near-antagonism. *Not* the way to treat a friend! And it is sad to hear one partner verbally exclude the other by talking about *my* house, or *my* bedroom, or *my* child.

Rebuild those early bonds by emphasizing the *we, us, our* in your relationship. For example, "*We* are going on vacation to Hawaii next month" or "This event will be a landmark move for *us*" and "*Our* daughter is planning to apply for a scholarship." When you speak of both of you in the familial plural, you begin to *think* of the two of you as an entity, to create and develop an awareness that both of you are a couple in feeling as well as in fact.

A happy, fulfilling relationship takes time and energy on the part of each person — whether the grouping consists of a man and a woman or an extended family.

By being open to the suggestions, hopes and desires of each other and tempering disagreements with a sense of humor and fair play, relationships can survive and grow. Sharing your life with another person is the ultimate commitment; loving and being loved in return are its greatest rewards. Enjoy!

Keep In Touch With The Child In Both You And Your Partner

♥ ♥ ♥ ♥ ♥

When a couple is searching for ways to get in touch with their fun-loving natures, to re-experience, together, the joy of discovery, the unadulterated happiness of being a child, the first step might be to look for situations that will recreate a semblance of that happy time.

Being around young children helps, of course, but that is not always possible given the mobility of families today. When a couple thinks back to the things that made childhood a special, magical time they might include catching fireflies on a July evening, wiener roasts, playing marbles or jumping rope, family picnics, roller-skating, waiting up for Santa Claus, sled riding—any number of simple pleasures that didn't involve a lot of time or money or effort, but just *were*.

In an attempt to re-create at least the remembrance of those feelings and, more importantly, to foster a return to more spontaneity, liveliness, pure fun and the joy of hopes and dreams in a relationship, the following suggestions reveal what other couples have found to be a window on that wonderful lost world—childhood time.

Spend a day playing like you did when you were kids.

Start your special "kids for a day" with a kid-pleasing breakfast of blueberry pancakes, maple syrup, and juice or hot chocolate. An adult cup of coffee may be needed to keep you from caffeine withdrawal! Dress in brightly colored casual wear and, if you can, fix your hair the way you wore it as a child. Top your outfit off with a backwards baseball cap—or your favorite fun headgear. Slip on your knapsacks and head for a nearby park—on foot or by bike. You are *kids*, remember? You don't drive! Spend some time on the swings and other equipment. Play a game or two of marbles, jacks, or hopscotch. If it is a windy day, assemble some kites and fly them. Race each other to a tree. Share peanut butter and jelly sandwiches. See who can blow the biggest bubbles.

Head for home and a hot shower in time to settle down to a big bowl of popcorn and a session of cartoon videos. Order in some kid-pleasing food for dinner. Later, when it's dark, if you have a yard or garden, sit in the grass and watch the fireflies. Magical! And there's still time for a game of hide-and-seek!

For the ultimate "kids day" spend a day or so at Disneyworld or a storybook theme park.

There are any number of specialized parks that cater to children and that offer a variety of activities that will appeal to couples who are looking for a way to get back in touch with their "inner child." After a day of being surrounded with fun rides, cartoon or storybook characters, and music geared to entertaining youngsters, the atmosphere is certain to have raised a couple's spirits. You can only smile at getting all sticky from eating spun-sugar candy or caramel-coated apples. And you both screamed with delight on the roller coaster, and were misty-eyed on the carousel.

Buy a few fun items to use later—like the "magic" wand with the glow-in-the-dark sparkles flowing through it. Use it

when granting special wishes—like baking a chocolate cake
or ???

Toy stores are not just for kids!

Nina and Len were walking by a giant toy store one afternoon. The lively window display attracted their attention, and
they decided to go into the store "just to look." Two hours
later the couple emerged, happy and laughing, each clutching
a bag of childhood delights.

Nina had chosen a game of jacks, which she hadn't played
since fourth grade. Len had a bag of marbles and a prize
"shooter." A jumping rope, a yo-yo, and a game of backgammon rounded out their purchases. They had such an enjoy-
able time buying and playing with their "toys" that they now
visit the store once a month.

Remember the yellow ducky you loved to have in the bathtub when you were a child? A whole flock of them can be great fun!

Cindy was very fond of little yellow ducks—the soft plastic
squeaky variety. One evening when she came home late from

work there was an envelope pinned to the door. Inside was a note inviting her to a "quackers only" party—in the bathroom! When she opened the bathroom door, she found a little table set with a tray of pâtés and crackers, a bottle of white wine in an ice bucket—and then she saw Larry, sitting in a tubful of floating yellow ducks! They had a "quackers" of a time!

Children's stories and fairy tales can be a great source of adult fun.

Try reading *The Three Bears*—with a grown-up twist. Perhaps it just wasn't the right chair or porridge or bed that Goldilocks was looking for! Acting out the parts of Little Red Riding Hood and the Big Bad Wolf can also be naughtily nice.

For a more romantic ending try *Sleeping Beauty* or *Snow White*. And what little girl hasn't dreamt of being Cinderella dancing with her Prince Charming? By using your imagination and being inventive, your adult versions of old favorites can result in a new appreciation of each other's "talents."

A great way for you and your partner to "chill out."

If you live in a climate where there is snow, save a big plastic bag of snowballs in the freezer. Choose a quiet evening when you are relaxing together in front of a fireplace, or listening to some favorite music. Tell your darling you have thought of a great way to "chill out." Further mystify your partner by placing a large rubber or plastic sheet on the floor in front of the fireplace. Your fur hat and mittens—and little else—are also intriguing. Time to bring out the snow! Use your imagination for loverly snow play, like shivery, tingly snowballs down his or her spine! Guaranteed to refresh a relationship suffering from the winter blahs.

Take gentle bondage a step further with this "teasing" scenario.

When you have tied your love gently with soft silk scarves, skate your fingertips over their erogenous zones. Follow this with a trail of light kisses. Sensational! Keep up the tension by doing a striptease. Of course, you are out of their reach—temporarily! What power! What *fun!*

Enjoying life to its fullest means letting go of unattainable "norms" and realizing your own achievements are small miracles in themselves.

When couples realize that happiness is not dependent on acquiring material things or reaching a certain "status," and concentrate instead on the joys of being together and experiencing the world around them through an awakened sense of their own worth, their relationship blooms.

Love is the most fragile yet the deepest and most enduring emotion human beings can experience. There is no richer life than one infused with love and its attendant devotion and caring. Cherish your relationship, fill it with the joyous wonder of a love that ennobles the soul even as it soars to the stars.

Romance, romance, romance: a relationship can never have too much of it.

Make use of every opportunity to show your love. Don't just glance at your darling, gaze deeply into his or her eyes and communicate soul to soul. Full-body hugs demonstrate your desire to be near your beloved, so use them often. Tell your darling he or she is important to you and show it by impromptu caring moments. These can be as simple as offering a special cup of coffee or as elaborate as a weekend alone at a luxurious hotel or a romantic bed-and-breakfast. It is the thought that counts—that and the loving message your voice, smile, and actions convey.

Learn the secret of "power kissing"!

Make your every kiss count. Hold that contact, gently increasing the pressure, for at least a slow count of twenty. Ditto with hugs and hand-holding. Make these loving gestures warmly passionate with the intensity you communicate by adding gentle pressure and increasing the length of these pleasurable contacts. Instead of just holding your partner's hand or arm, caress it. Make sure he or she realizes that *all* of his or her body is important to you.

To keep love alive and glowing, put your loved one first.

Love makes the world go 'round, and to keep yours spinning with love, let your partner know he/she is number one with you. This means always considering your loved one's needs and preferences when making plans—whether it is an evening out with friends or family or an upcoming vacation. Let your darling know, in no uncertain terms, that he/she is important to you, that you value his/her opinion and perhaps most importantly, you need and want his/her love. Realizing it is the two of you who form a unit, and that the rest of your world revolves around that twosome, will help you build a strong, love-centered life together.

Fun Bubbles For Lovers

♥ ♥ ♥ ♥ ♥

Having Fun and Laughing Together.

Having fun and laughing together is what every couple wants—and needs—to experience in their relationship. All too often, however, humor and lightheartedness fall victim to the demands of daily routine, the seriousness of building a career, the need to provide for a family, or the seemingly overwhelming crush and rush of daily living. Overcoming these obstacles and reestablishing a sense of fun can be a challenge—but a creative, renewing and highly stimulating one—for both of you!

There are hundreds of small, inexpensive ways to show your affection and express your feelings while enlivening your message with an exhilarating twist of fun and laughter. Whether you meet occasionally, are a steady twosome, or are in a committed relationship, your partner will appreciate these "fun bubbles" that add sparkle to your feelings for each other.

Just keep in mind how wonderful it will be to experience all those warm feelings that shared laughter brings to your relationship!

Start collecting cards, buttons, stickers—anything with a humorous message that reinforces your view of your partner as a fun person to be with.

Be on the lookout for funny sayings, hilarious cards, cartoons or humorous articles, buttons, T-shirts, stickers—any little thing that makes you smile or laugh—and collect them in a special box or folder. Then surprise your special friend by sending one of them from time to time by mail or placing items where they are sure to be found—on a pillow, in a pocket, taped to a mirror, in a briefcase, in an underwear drawer, and so on. People love to laugh—and love those who make them laugh!

Going for a long, boring drive? Be inventive and give the trip a surprise twist!

This fun idea works best on country roads or secondary roads—not on a superhighway! Look for a field of flowers, roadside blossoms, or bright autumn leaves. Pull over to the side of the road and gather a wild bouquet to present to your astonished love with a flourish and a kiss.

No flowers? No problem. Spin the radio dial to a station that is playing danceable music—the romantic kind. Choose a wide pulloff, turn the music up, and invite your surprised love to "trip the light fantastic" right there, by the side of the road! Be sure you have put the emergency brake and flashers on—you may be a while!

Give a workday breakfast a humorous touch!

Too early in the day for humor? Not at all. Serve chilled orange juice in champagne glasses and decorate with an edible flower or a luscious red strawberry. Drizzle a red jam heart on the toast, wear a silly hat and dark glasses and/or a black lace teddy. Offbeat? Yes—and definitely a morning brightener!

A morning hug is a great way to start the day.

A BIG bear hug the first thing in the morning gives your loved one a loving "warm fuzzies" feeling—and turns what seemed an impossible day into a *bear*able one.

Plan a "walkabout" dinner date that will take an entire evening and will provide a number of mementos for your "Romantic Souvenirs" collection.

Going out for dinner is always a treat, and this idea combines fun and collecting romantic souvenirs. You can adjust the types of places to suit your budget. The main thing is to enjoy yourselves for a long, romantic evening that you can look back on with pleasure and the warmth of shared laughter.

Start the evening off early with a late afternoon cocktail or cappuccino in a favorite lounge—preferably one up high or on the waterfront—with a view of the sunset. Take your time, flirt a little, relax. You have a whole evening ahead of you. A leisurely stroll brings you to the next stop: an intimate little place that serves great appetizers. Try a selection of spicy Spanish *tapas* or a variety of Lebanese or Greek hors d'oeuvres. You might also like to try the wines of the country represented. Ask the waiter to take a picture of the two of you. *Smile!*

Finished your appetizer? Time to move on to that elegant little—French?—restaurant where you have made reservations for a table in a secluded corner—or even in a private dining room! Of course you have checked that your favorite main dishes are on the menu and that the wine list is equal to the food! The candlelight and subdued lighting are so flattering—to both of you. The waiter won't mind taking your pictures and retrieving the wine label for you. Isn't this fun? And your thoroughly amused partner has no idea what you have planned for the next stop.

Dessert is undoubtedly expected, but first another leisurely walk—to a café famous for its fantabulous desserts. While you look over the extensive, calorie-rich menu, enjoy an espresso or sip a flute of champagne. Choosing a dessert is always fun and even more so when there are so many inspired concoctions tempting you. When you have decided on the perfect ending to your dining experience, you might want to ask for two forks to taste each other's "sweetness." Pictures, please!

The evening is approaching the Cinderella hour, so head over to that penthouse club that features dancing to live music. While you are waiting for the band to strike up your favorite tune, you and your love can watch the twinkling lights of the city in the distance as you linger over a relaxing herbal tea, coffee, or liqueur.

Dance the night away—and then it's time for a lovely pre-dawn breakfast buffet. Fresh juice, coffee, eggs Benedict, waffles (chocolate ones with strawberries and whipped cream garnish are memorable)—a feast fit for the end of a royally grand night to remember. Of course throughout that unforgettable night you have collected matchcovers, wine labels, photographs, swizzle sticks, cocktail napkins—no lamps or ashtrays, please!—that you can put in a special album or "Treasure Chest" (see end of this section) to look at over the years ahead, reliving the fun and laughter and love you shared on this memorable evening!

Starting a "Treasured Memories" collection.

When you have collected matchbooks, swizzle sticks, cocktail napkins, menus, ticket stubs, and photographs as mementos of pleasant evenings or special celebrations, take the time to organize this collection. Buy a large picture album, preferably one with a romantic cover and clear plastic pages. The next step is to organize your collection into separate events. Now you are ready to assemble the items on the proper page and to add comments—or mini–lovenote memories—with a colorful marker. Keep the album in a spot where you are likely to go through it often—such as on the coffee table or by your bedside. By remembering these happy occasions, you and your love can relive those magic moments of shared fun and laughter and rekindle the loving feelings you experienced at that time. Remembering these fun times is important to a relationship as it strengthens the bonds of love and acts as a reminder of your love when the two of you are going through a difficult time.

The album is also an incentive to add *more* happy times to your memories and mementos. Why not make a special effort to plan that next "memorable moment" *now*—and surprise your "treasure" with your thoughtfulness?

Do you have a poster of an event the two of you attended? Personalize it before having it framed.

Very often it is possible to buy a poster, playbill, or program of a musical, play, exhibition, or concert the two of you attended. Before having it framed, glue on special mementos: ticket stubs, photos of the two of you at the event or sharing a bite or drink before or after the show. Write your personal comments on the poster with colorful markers. If possible, have one or more of the performers autograph the item—perhaps even including a brief dedication to both of you. These little additions add a much more interesting touch and trigger happy, warm memories of a more personal nature every time you look at it.

♥ FOUR FUN THINGS YOU CAN DO TO ♥ KEEP YOUR LOVELIFE PERCOLATING WITH LAUGHTER:

♥ Disguise your voice using a favorite character or use a robotlike monotone in an unexpected phone call just to say "I miss you."

♥ Send a humorous note or card: It will lighten the dreariest day plus let your love know you are thinking of him or her.

♥ Wrap up a silly little gift like a trick mirror, a puzzle, a miniature game, a clown keychain—just to be thoughtful—and tuck it in your love's jacket pocket to be discovered later. Or slip it in a dinner napkin, a briefcase, or under a pillow. The surprise element is fun—for both of you!

♥ Plan a surprise picnic in a zany or unusual place: beside a fishpond in the park; in a deserted churchyard; in an old orchard amid blossoms in early spring; under a snow-covered gazebo in mid-winter; a bell tower with a fabulous view. Just make sure you have contacted the owners beforehand—an irate landowner appearing in the middle of an idyllic twosome would not be appreciated!

SIX MORNING BRIGHTENERS TO TRY:

♥ Draw a happy face on the bathroom mirror with shaving cream—or make lipstick hearts!

♥ Use a washable marker to draw hearts all over shower walls.

♥ Carve a heart in his soap-on-a-rope or on her beauty bar.

♥ Paste a rainbow sticker in a conspicuous place, like above the shower head or on a brush handle.

♥ Slip an I.O.U. for a dozen kisses and hugs into a bathrobe or pajama pocket.

♥ Stick a big I LOVE YOU! on top of the morning newspaper headlines

Breakfast al fresco!

If the morning is bright and sunny, why not have breakfast on the balcony or patio? Serve an exotic fruit with a humorous touch: Make a happy face with slices of banana—or whole strawberries—for eyes and a mango, cantaloup, or papaya slice for the mouth. Or arrange half a pineapple ring for a smile and use maraschino cherries for eyes. Slip a crazy straw and an edible flower into the fruit juice! Use your imagination to "start every day with a smile."

Add a touch of you to your love's lunch break!

Even if lunchtime is limited, there's time to meet for a quick sandwich and a soda or soft drink. A midday hug and kiss will lift anyone's spirits and make the afternoon go faster. This is not the time to discuss balancing the checkbook, however! Relax—and share a laugh.

When your schedule nixes sharing lunch, have a special "treat" delivered!

Is your day so rushed you have no time for lunch? Then have a fantastic lunch delivered to your love. There are caterers specializing in luncheon menus that offer quiches, an assortment of mini-sandwiches, exotic empanadas, samosas, cheese bites arranged on a pineapple, and fruits. Make sure a "Thinking of you—a lot!" card accompanies this special treat. Or perhaps a note like, "You're a feast to my eyes!" A little reminder of just how important and special he or she is to you!

Be the "hostess with the mostest!"

Surprise! Greet your love at the door as a waitress dressed in *really* skimpy attire—or as a waiter in "tuxedo" shorts. Say something like, "Good evening, I'm Millie, and I'll be waiting on you this evening." Offer a pre-dinner drink on a tray, and when he or she has recovered enough from all this attention to read, present a nicely designed menu—with a big kiss! Have the table set with your best china, stemware, and linens, and lots of lighted candles, of course, and fresh flowers, if possible.

Having seated your love with great ceremony, serve a beautifully garnished salad or other appetizer—perhaps a lip-shaped salmon mousse!—while you heat up the main dish, which you present on a nicely decorated platter. For dessert, you might like to offer an assortment of frosted minicakes arranged on lacy doilies, or a heart-shaped decorated cake—served with a kiss.

A special coffee in delicate china cups, accompanied by a sweet liqueur if you wish, adds a final touch of sentiment to this unexpected, romantic dining experience. It's a safe bet that the late, late show will feature clever *you!*

If the love of your life has ultraticklish feet, try a rose petal foot bath.

When your special person says no to a foot massage, smile sweetly and pamper him or her with this superbly delightful rose petal foot soother. Fill a basin with warm water and add a few drops of rose-scented essential oil or rose-water and several handfuls of soft rose petals. Then dab a few drops of the oil on your fingers and rub your blissful sweetheart's temples. Tension literally melts away!

Another great way to rev up the action and restore a flagging libido is an aphrodisiac rubdown!

You have read about the power of scent to set a mood, and this *scent*sual mixture makes the most of your darling's "nose for love"! *However, if your darling has allergies or sensitive skin, you might want to skip this one.*

Mix three drops of essential oil of jasmine, twelve drops of ylang-ylang, and an equal amount of sandlewood to a cup of pure aloe, almond oil, or an unscented baby oil. Have your darling warm his hands by rubbing them together—in delighted anticipation—and proceed to knead this magic potion into your willing body. Even nicer by candlelight!

Keep your love in the pink with a special bubble bath for two.

This pink-of-perfection bathing experience begins with a tubful of foaming rose-tinted and scented bath salts. Have lots of fluffy pink towels, washcloths, a pink bathmat, and matching pink robes if possible. Put soft pink-tinted lightbulbs in any lighting fixtures and add lots of pink candles. Or really go all out and add pink toothbrushes, pink toothpaste, toilet paper and pink-lensed sun glasses!

If you like, chill a bottle of pink champagne and have two tinted crystal flutes on a silver tray ready to toast your love. For music, "La Vie en Rose," of course! A few small bouquets of pink roses and rosebuds are extravagantly elegant. For a fabulous finale, sprinkle handfuls of pink rose petals over your bathing beauty and gently rub them into his skin. *Aaahh!* Perfection!

If your darling is a chocolate freak, this special bath is truly a treat.

Didi loved chocolate—in any form. One of her wildest fantasies was to bathe in a tubful of chocolate milk. Her husband decided that, as an unusual treat for her birthday, he would fulfill this dream. He decided on the full chocolate treatment: chocolate shaped candles, a box of Godiva chocolates by the tub, a steaming cup of hot chocolate, and a tub filled with hot chocolate. He used several large boxes of skim milk powder and mixed the chocolate powder with them, added hot water, poured in a quart of real cream, and squirted an entire can of whipped cream on top. He led his blindfolded darling to the tub and lovingly undressed her before he let her see the tub of chocolate. They had a very sensuous time eating chocolates, squirting each other with whipped cream, and luxuriating in the chocolate bath!

One of the latest bathing delights has a special "oceanic" touch.

If your "water baby" loves the scent of the sea, treat him or her to a special soak in "blue caviar"—a bath bead packed with skin-pampering oils—from Vitabath. Towels scented with a refreshing men's cologne are a nice touch. Blue light also would be relaxing.

This refreshing yet soothing bath is sublime for hot summer days.

Float handfuls of lime and lemon slices in the bath water. Light citrus-scented summer sherbet candles, pile a stack of soft yellow towels by the tub, and soothe tired eyes with cotton balls dipped in cool Perrier. Provide large glasses of iced fresh lemonade for sipping while relaxing and meditating on the good things life has brought your way—like your relationship!

Try this jiggly, squiggly "cooling off" tip for a sizzle rating on the romance thermometer!

In the middle of the good old summertime when the temperature is hot and getting cool is more important than getting it on, fill the bathtub with semi-chilled blue jello. Keep the blue theme going with blue towels, light bulbs, candles, soaps, and flowers. Invite your sweetie to share the "blues" with you—you might even have funky blue jazz music playing in the background. Or challenge your love to a "Jell-O wrestling match"—in the tub. Hilarious! Finish off with a shower à deux!

Create an oasis of fun in a rushed day.

You both have hectic schedules and long days. But you want to see each other, somehow. Why not plan to meet for a late afternoon "sweetness break"—ice cream, hot chocolate, or cake and coffee—at a favorite café or hotel? Share a joke, flirt a little, play "footsie," kiss passionately and head for that evening lecture or association meeting refreshed—and smiling!

A spa can be a great relationship strengthener.

At Le Sport in St. Lucia, honeymoon couples learn how to give each other neck and back rubs as well as share a wide range of specialty services like herbal bodywraps, facials, hydrotherapy and other stress-relievers. These couples experience the openness and closeness that can only come through being relaxed and vulnerable—together!

If you can't get away to an exotic spa, spend a pampering day together at home.

The everyday bath, shave and shampoo become special and indulgent when you share these activities. Stock up on those nice beauty items you've been wanting to try: a peppermint and eucalyptus shaving cream, an oatmeal/almond exfoliant, a coconut-oil-based scalp massage lotion, mud packs, luxuriously rich shampoos. Giving your darling a shave and a shampoo is a caring activity—and fun! Add a shiatsu massage while you shampoo his hair. Lather the hair and gently rest your fingers on his forehead while you apply pressure to the temples with your thumbs. Gradually, to a count of six, release this pressure. Repeat this process ten to fifteen times. Very relaxing!

Both of you can have a great time trying out the exfoliants and mud packs. Yes, men like all this beauty stuff when it helps them to look better, too! Follow up with a hair trim— if you dare!

A manicure and pedicure—even men like clear nail polish on fingers and toes—complete with a mint-scented hand and foot massage is a wonderful ending to your mutual "beauty session." Add a small cloth dipped in warm rose-water to reduce eye tiredness. Apply these to your darling's closed eyelids while you do his/her nails.

Home entertainment possibilities are only limited by your imagination. A warm shower or an herbal-scented bath—perhaps with floating candles?—rounds out your beauty night ritual. Slipping into silky nightwear for both of you adds to the sensuous, spoiled-to-death feeling. Soothed and pampered, you and your partner are ready for a sensual session of mutual love-giving that gives new meaning to the saying "Good night"!

Add a touch of the Orient to your "home spa" with these exotic suggestions.

There is a marvelous spa in Bangkok where you can luxuriate in a papaya body polish. If tripping off to the Oriental Spa Thai Health and Beauty Center situated in the spectacular multi-award winning Oriental Hotel on the banks of the Chao Phraya River in Bangkok would give your travel budget a permanent stress fracture, head for your local fruit market and stock up on papayas, mangoes and bananas. A quick whir in the blender and you are ready to outdo the nimble-fingered masseuse who uses the fresh fruit pulp to exfoliate and smooth the bodies of the totally pampered spa guests. This particular body soother is touted as the Jet Lag Solution and can be combined with a hydrotherapy session—think sinking into a warm bath. Dip cotton balls in blueberry flower water and place on their closed eyelids to reduce tiredness and puffiness.

Add aromatherapy massage—you can substitute with a lemon or rose-based essential oil—for pure bliss. It's the perfect way to greet your darling when he returns from a long flight—or a stressful work day!

Remember how much you loved a secret? Here's a great one the two of you can share!

When your love is getting dressed, sneak up and plant a big lipstick kiss on his chest. Or his lower back, or ??? Only the two of you will know it's there! His secretive, silly grin will drive everybody insane with wanting to know what's making him so happy. Promise him a dozen more kisses—his choice of where!—if he doesn't tell!

Tattoos are all the rage today—and it doesn't have to be a permanent one to be effective!

Surprise your loved one with a discreet temporary tattoo of his or her name—perhaps on that tip of your shoulder blade where a kiss gives you so much pleasure. Even more fun if you use a nickname known only to the two of you!

Create a room within a room for an evening with a difference!

Have you just read a novel about desert sheiks and veiled women? Want to transport some of that exotic world into your own? Transform a spare bedroom or a part of another large room into a tented paradise.

Collect a stack of colorful throw rugs—Orientals, whether real or imitation, are great. Add incense burners, low tables, large floor cushions, a big futon. Your friends' and relatives' basements and attics are a good place to look for these items.

Put some hooks in the ceiling at the points where you want to drape your "tent" from, and using huge white sheets, fashion your "desert retreat."

If the two of you prefer a more rustic environment, use the same tent idea to create a "camping" escape.

For this miniretreat, put folding camp cots or a double air mattress in the tent, a low, folding table for munchies, and a Coleman lantern for soft lighting. Stick some glow-in-the-dark stars on the ceiling of the room and inside the tent. For a woodsy touch, spray the room with pine scent. Load a cassette player with tapes of bird song and other wildlife sounds. Or if you want a safari theme, spray a musky scent and play jungle music and African drums. Why not eat a "camp dinner" in your rustic setting? Dress the part by wearing camping gear or sexy "Me Tarzan, you Jane" outfits. Jungle print underwear adds to the atmosphere! It's great fun to pretend to be scared by a wild animal and need to be protected and comforted by your own passionate beast! Rowr!

For sweet dreams, keep contention and other negative vibes out of the bedroom. Even better, outside the home.

Every couple has disagreements—minor to major. Try to hold verbal spats in some prearranged quiet spot. Vicky and Norman chose the middle of the woods. They lived in town, but not far from a heavily wooded area. They had made an agreement to head for the woods when tensions rose. Sometimes they would even go in separate cars to meet at an old sugar shack surrounded by acres of sugar maples. There were metal buckets to sit on—or to kick in frustration—and only the wild animals to hear their argument. More often than not, their angry words ended in a grin at a quizzical squirrel or a vociferous bluejay. Just walking together in the fresh air seemed to dissipate many of their spats. And when hurts or disappointments were really serious, they knew they could talk them out without leaving angry feelings or emotions floating around the rooms they shared at home. Look for a place to hold your "peace-making" sessions. How about a deserted stage? An old cemetery where you can "bury" your injured feelings? Be as original and inventive as you like: a peaceful home environment will be your reward.

Revitalize a humdrum, ho-hum, and generally boring week with this innovative calendar.

Take a fairly large piece of white cardboard and glue a picture of a couple hugging and kissing on the top section. Use one of you and your love if available. Mark the rest of the page into seven large segments and label them with days of the week. Now comes the fun part. On each of these segments write a short note of something you are going to do for—or to—your significant other on that day and cover each with a tear-off label. Be mysterious: Don't tell everything!

Example: The Sweet Fairy will strike at 7 PM. Be there!

For this one, put on a silky robe, fashion a fairy wand, and serve a decadently fabulous cake accompanied by a flute of champagne. Declare a "sweet time" and follow up with a sugary kiss!

You can use previous tips from this section or invent your own "minidiversions" to intrigue and thrill your love for the rest of the week. No peeking at the next day's surprise!

Are you puzzled by your love's behavior but don't want to comment? Try this trick to reveal his thoughts.

Draw a large heart on red paper and write on it with a black marker: YOU ARE A PUZZLE TO ME. Cut the heart into zigzag sections, like puzzle pieces, and mail them to him in a scented envelope. When he assembles them and reads your note, he will undoubtedly laugh and be more receptive to discussing what's bothering him.

Business trip coming up? Keep the home fires burning— by video!

When you have to be away for an extended period, make a minivideo that tells your dear one how much you love him or her. Have your favorite song playing in the background. Talk about the fun you share and how much being together means to you. Add a sexy or fun touch by gradually undressing as you talk. When you are nearly down to the altogether—excepting underwear and a hat—walk toward the camera as though entering an embrace. Fade to black.

No video camera? Put it all on tape!

The message is the message after all! It would be so nice for the love of your life to be able to listen to a cassette of your voice telling of your love while beautiful music fills the background. A *lovely* way to fall asleep—to dream of thoughtful you!

Picture yourself on a shirt or tie!

In nearly every large shopping mall you can find a kiosk where you can have a photograph printed on an article of clothing. See how long it takes for your love to notice you are wearing his or her picture!

You can also make use of this technique by having your love's photo copied onto a piece of material that you then sew into a blazer or jacket. Then you can truly say he or she is always near your heart!

Keep your romance alive and vital by being courteous and thoughtful **every day,** *not just on special occasions.*

It's the everyday courtesies and little thoughtful gestures that add up to a vibrant, ongoing romance. Try to do at least two things each day that show your loved one that you care. Something as simple as seating your "best girl" at the table each evening, for example.

Marvin has performed this gentle, courteous gesture for Diane every time they share a meal—even for breakfast! Arranging a chair for the one you love is a simple act, but it reinforces the feeling that you value her presence and want to take care of her.

Daniel has served breakfast in bed to Nicole every morning for the past 30 years! He prepares it himself and serves it on a silver tray—even if it's only orange juice, toast and coffee! What a wonderfully pampered way to start the day!

Here are a few more ideas that apply to both men and women:

♥ Prepare a soothing bubble bath for your love when he comes home tired from work.

♥ Massage neck and shoulders or offer a foot massage.

♥ Put your arm around her or slip his hand through your arm when walking together.

♥ Butter the breakfast toast for her.

♥ Cut out articles you know your love would like, or slip little things for a favorite stamp or matchbook collection under his breakfast napkin.

♥ Buy your mate's favorite magazine the first day it is on the newsstands.

Simple things, but they all add up to a big dose of CARING!

Intimate little puzzles are also great fun to make and send.

Write a love message (or glue a cartoon or your picture with a LOVE YOU written on it) on heart-shaped heavy paper or cardboard. Cut it into jigsaw-type pieces and mail it to your love's office. Or tuck the envelope in a suitcase, gym bag, pocket, or briefcase. This little diversion won't leave your sweetie "puzzled" about your affections!

Another "puzzling" surprise!

Write a love poem on a piece of cardboard—legibly, please!—and cut it into puzzle pieces and mail it to the one you adore—but leave out a major piece. Don't sign your name. Of course he will call and ask you about it, but pretend you know nothing. When he is really confused, recite the poem in its entirety!

Playing games together gives you a great chance for added fun and laughs.

Even competitive board games, like Scrabble, can become a joint effort if you bend the rules a little. Try for the highest combined score, for example. Do the same when playing backgammon, chess, darts, cards, mah-jongg, etc.

Invent your own version of Trivial Pursuit with paper hearts and silly questions or statements like "This song was playing on the radio when we first kissed." "Your Mom was wearing a _____ dress when you introduced me." This is a great way to relive—in detail—those almost-forgotten good times together.

Those times of the year when there are "star showers" can be memorable for both of you.

Watch the newspapers or consult an almanac for those dates when showers of stars (actually, meteorites falling and burning as they enter earth's atmosphere) are to be visible. Plan a late-night-under-the-stars camp-out complete with a comfy sleeping bag for two. Cuddled together under an open sky, waiting for the stars to fall, is a *lovely* bonding experience!

Present your love with a certificate naming a star after him or her.

Of all the seemingly numberless stars in the heavens, you can arrange to have one named for your favorite person. The International Star Registry will send you a map designating the location of the star and a certificate stating that a particular star bears your darling's name. They can be contacted at:

The International Star Registry
Dept. 1001
34523 Wilson Road
Ingleside, IL 60041
Telephone: (800) 282-3333

You can also choose a pair of stars that revolve around each
other and have them named for the two of you. What could
be more romantic that looking up at a star-filled sky and
picking out your own star or stars? An International Star Certificate is the perfect gift for any occasion when you want to
show a loved one how very special he or she is.

Surprise your partner with a night at the beach — in the living room!

Set the stage with sun umbrellas, folding chairs, a portable radio, bright lights, a sun lamp, and self-tanning creams. Have
tall pitchers of lemonade or iced tea on hand, and a video of a
beach movie. Drape the furniture with white sheets.

Open the door wearing a bathing suit—your sexiest, of
course—sunglasses, and a floppy straw hat salvaged from last

year's trip to the islands. Have reggae music booming in the background. It would add to the fun if you can get a couple of friends to drop in dressed in the same style.

No cooking. This is a *beach*! Order in a Hawaiian pizza and enjoy a potent planter's punch, piña colada, or banana daiquiri while waiting for the delivery boy. Aloha!

Do you want to tell the whole world how much someone means to you? Defacing trees is not only old hat, it harms the environment. Try something more unusual.

Dwayne wanted everyone to know how much he loved Alice. But she was a very private person and wasn't comfortable with public displays of affection until the day Dwayne pulled this stunt!

He took a piece of ordinary blackboard chalk, drew a huge heart, and wrote I LOVE YOU, ALICE in big letters on the asphalt driveway of their house. Alice loved his declaration so much, she wouldn't let anyone park in the driveway for a whole week!

Another way to announce your passion for someone is via the electronic highway.

If you have access to electronic bulletin boards through your computer, choose one your partner often signs onto and leave your love message "on the board."

You can also set up your love's computer screen to flash your love message when the set is turned on. Nice way to start a working day!

Or use e-mail to leave a message on your special person's private computer mailbox. More personal than a fax—as long as you don't mistakenly put the message on a network system that the whole office can access!

When there has been a heavy snowfall, show your love in spades!

Lisa was dreading having to shovel her driveway and clean the snow off her car. When she was ready to leave for work she was delighted and surprised to find a note on her door. "To my darling Snow Queen: Your car is clean—and ditto the driveway. Have a nice day. Your faithful servant, Leopold." What a lovely way to show you care!

Humorous "rewards" are marvelous incentives.

When your sweetie has done something particularly helpful or thoughtful, reward him or her—and yourself!—with a choice of something fun from a box of humorous gag items you have collected and wrapped for such an occasion. It might be a little plaque with a funny saying, or a cute bookmark, a puzzle keychain, a miniature bottle labeled APHRODISIAC, or a check for a dozen kisses and a big hug. How about a ticket for a fun ride at an amusement park? Tickets to a comedy show? Use your imagination: Fun and laughter spring from shared humor, not an expensive bauble.

Kidnap your love for a fabulous evening or weekend.

Arrange to pick your love up from work. Once seated in the car—or chauffeured limo, if you can afford it—slip a blindfold over their eyes and announce that they have been kidnapped for the rest of the evening. While you drive (or are driven) to a secret destination, your "captive" may try to guess where the two of you are headed. No peeking allowed!

Your destination may be as simple as the place where you first kissed; a favorite restaurant with "your" table reserved; a quiet lakeside picnic; a whopping banana split at an old-fashioned ice cream parlor. The choice is yours, the anticipation and surprise are for sharing!

Create a romantic boudoir for intimate moments.

A bedroom can be the most boring room in your life—or it can be transformed into a romantic retreat—all it takes is a little ingenuity and some paint and fabric.

The simplest bed can be given a luxurious setting with drifts of fine tulle or lace hung from ceiling hooks. For a more opulent look, search for old brocade or velvet drapes. Cover a table with a floor-length cloth and add a vase of silk flowers and a delicate lamp. Wall-to-wall carpeting that you detest? Buy a mill-end remnant that will cover most of it, or use several medium-sized Oriental rugs. Large floor cushions and a low table for cosy cups of tea or a glass of wine are nice additions. The idea is to make the room look inviting with the bed as a focal point. It is worth it to splurge on a beautiful quilt or comforter that will give your spirits a lift every time you enter the room. If you stick to white or cream linens, it is easier to add color in choosing the rest of your furnishings.

Why not try a small, imitation Persian rug as a dresser scarf instead of the usual flimsy ones? Glass can be cut to measure for a modern touch, or use mirrored squares for a bright, fresh look.

With all the antiquing kits and colorful enamels on the market, there is no need to have expensive, elaborate chests and tables. Secondhand "finds" can be personalized and dramatized with paint and unusual hardware. Be eclectic. Treasured items on display are inviting and make a room more intimate.

A Tiffany lamp or a real candelabra is a nice touch. Just be careful not set the candles where they will ignite anything or be too close to a smoke detector. Setting off a fire alarm is not a recommended prelude to an intimate evening!

Swing through life together — really!

Remember those wonderful long wooden swings that used to hang on wide front or back porches? And the swoonderful summer evenings you spent swinging gently with a special someone? Even if you don't have a wide porch, you can hang a swing on a tree. Conversation seems to flow easier when you are gently swaying with your head on a dear one's shoulder. It's like dancing—sitting down!

Keeping the "magic" going in a relationship takes more than an "illusion" of caring.

Show your love how much you care for them by doing small things that may not seem overly romantic on the surface, but that add up to BIG CARING. For example, give your significant other a relaxing shoulder/neck massage while encouraging them to tell you about their day or problems they are facing. These few moments of sharing and caring are worth more to the stability and depth of a relationship than hundreds of bottles of expensive perfumes and rooms full of roses.

Make some cardboard "tokens" to be "accepted as loving tender."

Take a piece of thin white cardboard and draw several two-inch-diameter circles on it. Write things like "Good for a long walk in the moonlight," "Good for a candlelight dinner," "Good for one full hour of attention," or a massage, a game of Scrabble, a trip to the art gallery—for all those little things the one you love really likes and appreciates. Put them in a decorative little box and place it where your love will be sure to find it. Your thoughtfulness and willingness to do those things you recognize are important to the one you care about will enrich your relationship more than elaborately expensive gifts.

Any time you greet the love of your life with a kiss, hold it!

Keeping a kiss going for ten seconds—minimum—turns this fleeting contact into an act of love and caring. It gives you time to "connect" better after having been apart, even for a short time. Try it. Count up to fifteen, slowly, silently—then keep stretching the time until you get it up to at least half a minute. An improved relationship is on its way with every second of increase!

Just *try* frowning after someone has kissed you for thirty or forty seconds!

Take advantage of opportunities for making a royally romantic gesture.

It is surprising how often romantic fantasies involve limousines and champagne. Make use of this fact to plan a romantic gesture that will keep the light in your love's eyes burning bright—at least until jet lag hits them!

When your loved one is returning from an extended business trip, you want to show how lonely you were *in a big way.* This is the perfect opportunity to rent a white stretch limo, fill it with flowers, add a bottle of chilled champagne—and terrific-looking you. To be sure they'll see you when they clear customs and enter the arrival lounge, wave a big "welcome home" heart-shaped balloon with their name on it! Five star reciprocal reception guaranteed!

Add a touch of the "Cinderella Factor" for a fun twist to dining out.

Jean Claude was always thinking up practical jokes to keep Diane amused. Like mixing bubble gum balls in with her bubble bath beads, or slipping her funny notes when she was arguing with her brother over the phone. One evening when they were dining at their favorite restaurant with a few friends, Diane removed her high-heeled shoes as she often did when seated. While Diane was busy talking to her girlfriend who was sitting next to her, Jean Claude managed to retrieve the shoes without Diane's noticing. Then Jean Claude excused himself, and, hiding the shoes from Diane's view, pretended to head for the washroom. When dinner was over, Diane searched under the table for her shoes and was dismayed when she couldn't locate them. Just then all twelve waiters solemnly marched in and the headwaiter presented the shoes to her on a silver serving tray! Diane's embarrassment turned to delighted surprise when she discovered a beautifully wrapped little package sticking out of one of the shoes. In it was a diamond bracelet with a note: "To my Cinderella from her Prince!"

Of course, you needn't include a diamond bracelet: It's the thought that counts!

Surprise your love with an "it isn't Christmas but—" stocking.

You've been browsing through a department store or a dollar store or ogling the cosmetic counters and you've collected all these really neat little samples and small gifts. Only it isn't anywhere near your love's birthday, and it isn't Christmas. Just for fun, fill a big Christmas stocking or a white tube sock (stick its mate in the toe) with the assortment of goodies you've found and hang it on the mantel or put it under a pillow or hide it under the morning newspaper. Great fun way to start—or end—a day!

Do you know how to embroider or to make use of any other decorative art? Use your talents to express your love.

What would be nicer when taking a nap or watching TV than to have an embroidered or tapestry pillow or cushion to rest against—particularly when it bears a love message! Entwined hearts with MARY LOVES TOM or YOU ARE MY SUNSHINE! or a cupid motif—any design that includes your names and a romantic touch will be a loving message communicated every time the article is used.

Another nice touch is a pair of silk pajamas embroidered with your love's initials. Add a heart in a strategic location or two—for fun!

Look for zany articles of clothing, like this one.

Corrine was walking past a department store window when she did a double-take! On display was a two-headed T-shirt with wild love messages written all over it. She couldn't resist buying one, and that evening she and Fred were walking around laughing like two crazy kids in their T-for-two!

Try this tip to "warm up" a "cold" romance.

Everyone likes to get into a nice, warm, comfy bed on chilly nights. Warm up the love of your life by warming up his or her sleeping spot. Either lie there yourself for a few minutes just before bedtime or tuck a large hot water bottle between the sheets. A really thoughtful touch is to warm favorite nightwear in the clothes dryer and slip it under the pillow.

Treat your treasure to a "Love-is-a-money-splendored-thing" experience.

There is a scene in the movie *Indecent Proposal* where the married couple spreads the money that was given to them all over the bed in their hotel room. Recreate this erotic rite by spreading a hundred—or more, if you wish—crisp, new bills over your best satin sheets while your unsuspecting sweetie is taking a bath.

Light up your lovelife — literally!

Turn an ordinary little flashlight into a sensuous love toy. After "lights out," use your flashlight to spotlight various sections of your love's anatomy describing in detail what you are going to do to each part. Bet it won't be long before your love grabs a flashlight and the "light wars" are *on*!

Sing your own song of love.

With today's technology, it is possible to make a music video of yourself singing a love song. Get a good friend to help. Using a standard video camera and a music-only cassette for accompaniment, supply your own words or make sure to substitute the name of your loved one where possible. If you can't carry a tune, chose your favorite love song and lip sync. You may also want to precede the song with a personalized message. Choosing the music, props, outfit, and moves is a fun project—and the results will thrill that special person in your life!

Play poor, little, wounded person and get a kiss for every Band-aid!

Lena was putting a Band-aid on a cut finger, when she had a brilliant idea. She had a lot of Band-aids of all sizes and a lot of places she would like to have kissed and made "better." Tim was surprised to find Lena wearing a bikini and a lot of Band-aids when he arrived for their evening out. By the time he had kissed all her "hurts," they were having so much fun they spent the evening at home—in bed! He, as the "doctor," prescribed at least an hour of "bed rest"!

Suggest a late evening walk and end with a relaxing drink.

Whatever the weather—a light summer rain or new-fallen snow—suggest a late night walk to experience the elements. When you return home, prepare a hot, fragrant herbal tea sweetened with honey and serve it in your fanciest cups. Or offer a warming cordial served in delicately etched glasses. An elegant contrast to the wilder weather you experienced together—and the tempestuous moments ahead!

Add a touch of the spiritual to the blessings of your togetherness.

Whether or not you are a member of a religious organization, you can give the spiritual dimension of your natures a lift by simply going for a long walk in the woods or mountains or meadows together—in silence. By learning to meditate and to experience the quiet and peace of your inner selves, you will emerge from these experiences strengthened in your resolve to share your lives on many levels and to expand your openness to each other.

To keep those wonderful, bubbly feelings you experienced when you first fell in love, treat each other like lovers-in-love.

It is so easy to let routine and daily cares erode the loving feelings that brought a couple together in the first place. Overcome this tendency by actively reminding yourself that you want this person with whom you are sharing your life to fall in love with you again and again. How can you make this happen? By treating that special person in your life like he or she *is* special—and very loved. Think of your partner as a lover, as someone with whom you want to explore and learn and grow—and realize it will take a lifetime to do this! In this way, you will also take the time to make yourself interesting, to encourage the love you want to receive, to look for ways to make your relationship work, and to continually rediscover and recreate the sense of "magic" in your love for each other. This doesn't mean that every day will be all sunshine and roses, but it keeps the natural lows from undermining the significantly rewarding highs you encounter. By making use of the information in this book, you will keep the attraction, fun, and laughter—and love—flowing between you.

Memorable Holiday Celebrations

♥ ♥ ♥ ♥ ♥

The holidays are a perfectly *lovely* reason to celebrate the occasion and your love! Try the suggestions in this chapter to stimulate your own creativity, to give those special events in your life a loving touch of thoughtfulness and caring. When you take the time and make the effort to create an atmosphere of fun and happiness, you will be rewarded with a lovelife that is rich and vibrant, satisfying and joyful.

♥ NEW YEAR'S EVE ♥

Make New Year's resolutions that will keep your love bright.

Instead of just making resolutions that are forgotten the next day or week, put together a calendar that will make sure you keep those "loving" resolutions. Take a regular calendar and glue a picture of the two of you on the top section. Use little sticker symbols and hearts to remind each other of kisses, hugs (a teddy bear), special pampering like a massage (a tiny rainbow, perhaps), stars—!, special occasions like birthdays (candles on a cake or balloons), anniversaries (don't forget to celebrate the day you met!), whatever represents things you want to remember and to express throughout the year. Put something on every date—even if it's just a hug, kiss, and smile—preferably all three! Looking at the calendar daily will remind you to express your love in some way, however small, and will keep the significant person in your life reminded of major events like anniversaries and birthdays without your having to say a word. This is *not* the calendar on which to write parent/teacher meetings and dentist appointments!

Another great New Year's idea is a "personalized" agenda for his or her briefcase.

Buy an ordinary day calendar and add your own little notes here and there. Include love notes, "I think you're terrific!" notes, birthday and anniversary reminders, funny stickers, bits of poetry, or lines about love from books of quotations. Glue a picture of yourself—or the two of you—inside the front cover and a love poem inside the back cover. These serendipitous little messages are truly "day brighteners," plus they give your loved one the added daily pleasure of an extra-personal touch from thoughtful you!

♥ VALENTINE'S DAY CELEBRATIONS ♥
FOR SWEETHEARTS ♥

Of all the days of the year, the fourteenth of February is traditionally the one set aside to celebrate romance. Candy and flowers and sentimental cards are standard fare and certainly lovely to give and receive, but for something unusual, inventive, and out of the ordinary, try one or more of the following innovative ideas.

Record your love letter on a CD.

This expression of your love takes some planning. Begin by writing down all those loving, complimentary things you want to tell the love of your life. You can go on at length, as the average CD runs approximately twenty minutes. Read your letter out loud, slowly, clearly—noting how long your message takes. When you actually record the words, have your valentine's favorite love songs playing in the background. This unusual, sentimental, personalized gift will be sure to please your heart's delight. You either can ask a friend who has the special recording equipment to do this for you, or inquire at your local record or CD player store for information.

For a shorter message, Hallmark cards now offer cards with built-in recording disks for a brief, personal message that plays when the card is opened!

Try this delight for sweet "pillow talk!"

Choose a heart-shaped box of luxurious Swiss or Belgian chocolates or wrap a small box of her favorite sweets in special Valentine's Day motif paper and slip it under her pillow. Sweet dreams guaranteed!

Declare your love publicly: Send a personal message via the Valentine Lovelines message page in your local newspaper.

Many newspapers print personal love messages for Valentine's Day. Check with the classified department of your local paper. Prices vary according to the length of the message and whether graphics are included. You could even try a few lines of loving, romantic poetry.

This special "remembrance from the heart" will surely thrill your valentine!

There is nothing more special than a highly personalized expression of love. And what could be more individual than the feelings you had for each other when you first met? Your very own *Love Story*?

Choose a beautiful, large, book-sized card that has several blank pages in it—or add pages to one yourself—and describe in your own words the beginning of your lovelife together. Include all the details of where and how you met, the weather, the clothing, perfume and aftershave or cologne you both wore, and—very important—your feelings for your loved one at this romantic first meeting. This wonderfully sentimental gift will be treasured by your darling and may well become a family heirloom.

Have your special Valentine's Day greeting mailed from Valentine, Nebraska!

To surprise your darling, send your card, with the envelope pre-addressed and stamped, in a covering envelope to Postmaster, Valentine, Nebraska. Look for other places on the map to have holiday cards mailed from: Bethlehem, Pennsylvania, for example, for Christmas.

♥ ST. PATRICK'S DAY ♥

Celebrate the luck of the Irish — even if you can't claim Irish heritage!

The wearing of the green is one of the more visible aspects of St. Patrick's Day, as are the parades in major cities throughout North America and the British Isles. Even in the world famous Raffles Bar in Singapore, a special Irish Mist drink is served to patrons on March 17! Treat your favorite Irish lad or lass to a shamrock decorated cake or a pot of shamrocks for his or her desk. Or choose a merry leprechaun to entice smiles from your dimpled darling. Is there a store in your area that handles Irish imports? Matching Irish fisherman's sweaters in kelly green wool or cotton are a great way to "show your colors!"

♥ EASTER CELEBRATIONS WITH A ♥ DIFFERENCE

Easter is a time for renewal, a reawakening of your deepest feelings of love, and the perfect time for a touch of light-hearted fun. Make the most of that feeling of newness, of spring rain freshness, a delight in the return of brighter, longer days, gentler breezes and the first flowers of the season. This is a time to bless your relationship with a fresh, light, fun-filled approach to your expressions of love.

Painting Easter eggs is a fine tradition. Take it a step further with this unique suggestion.

Remember the fun you had dying and painting Easter eggs when you were a child? Capture the creativity and fun of that activity by applying your talent to body-painting! Using non-toxic face-painting colors (often found in toy stores), paint hearts, stars, bunnies, love words, flowers, leaves—anything you like—on your love's body. Looking for different ideas? You can use tattoo design books for inspiration. Adding to the fun, painting some body areas really and truly tickles! Everything washes off easily in tub or shower—why not scrub-a-dub à deux?

Miniature chocolate Easter eggs can lead your love on a trail to your heart.

Give your favorite "Easter Bunny" a paper-grass-lined Easter basket. Tell your love that in a few minutes the great Treasure Egg Hunt will begin, but first to close his or her eyes tightly and wait for your signal to open them. Using a big bag of foil-wrapped chocolate minieggs, leave a trail of "eggs" to a room you have chosen for the "Grand Finale!" Decorate this room with big tulle bows and baskets of spring flowers. If you have chosen a bedroom, you might want to use lavender satin sheets and cases on the bed, scented with a light floral perfume. The idea is to have a fresh, spring atmosphere as the setting. To add to the decor, wrap yourself with a wide ribbon band with the word TREASURE spelled out in gold stick-on letters. Either drape yourself in a comfy chair or strike a pose on the bed. Announce that the hunt is now open. You will probably be finding little chocolate eggs all over the place for days to come because your love dropped the basket when he or she saw the "Treasure!" Happy hunting!

♥ LABOR DAY ♥

Labor day is* the *day to labor for your love.

Wherever you live, give Labor Day your own special meaning by declaring it an official day for labors of *love*. Begin the pampering with a lovely breakfast served in bed, complete with cinnamon-flavored cappuccino and strawberries dipped in chocolate. Present your love with a card declaring that you will be his or her love laborer for the day, and that your love's slightest wish is your command.

You can be sure this will be a busy day! Among the many pleasant duties that can arise could be reading love poems aloud, feeding luscious chocolates to your love, reading the funnies out loud, preparing an elaborate brunch, anything your nearest and dearest thinks will make him or her feel completely pampered. You might even present a list of things you would be delighted to do and let your love choose. Happy laboring for love!

♥ HALLOWEEN ♥

Although Halloween was originally a "hallowed eve," a time to revere the spirits of the dead, the day has become a fun-filled occasion.

With its ghosts and goblins, pumpkin jack-o-lanterns and drifts of spiderwebs, Halloween parties offer the perfect opportunity to add a bit of mystery and magic to your lovelife. A costume party where everyone is masked is a great way to rediscover the attraction you and your loved one have for each other. Just make sure you aren't flirting outrageously with the wrong person!

It's great fun to dress up and make the rounds of the neighborhood as a couple. Trick-or-treating knows no age barriers!

This is also the traditional time to visit a fortune-teller, consult astrologers, have your Tarot cards or palms read, even play with an Ouija board. Your sense of humor and willingness to join in the "spirit" of the occasion will help you through those moments when the "seer" proclaims that your love will meet a tall, dark, handsome stranger and *you* are a *blond!*

Even if you aren't having a party, carve up a bunch of pumpkins as a surprise for the love of your life.

Just looking at a gap-toothed pumpkin face is laugh-provoking. Imagine what a whole tribe of them would look like! Go to your local farmer's market and buy a lot of pumpkins in all different sizes and carve a wide range of facial expressions on them. If you have an assortment of wigs, old hats, or scarves, you can even add those to "flesh out" the pumpkin characters. Carefully place thick candle stubs in each lantern for maximum effect. Arrange them along the porch and down the steps, or set them aglow throughout the house and turn out the lights. What a terrific background for a "thrilling" intimate moment!

Midnight can be wonderfully, scarily magical by the glow of jack-o'-lanterns.

Why not fill your living room or bedroom with lighted orange candles and glowing, small, carved pumpkins? Add a chocolate fondue and feed each other small, sweet tangerine sections dipped in the chocolate while you cuddle up and tell ghost stories to each other or listen to a recorded scary story or watch a horror movie on a black and white TV. Potent love magic for those who relish a slight shiver running up and down their spine! Boris Karloff masks and glow-in-the-dark skeleton pajamas? Mickey and Minnie Mouse costumes? Really?! Oh well, whatever turns you on!

Halloween is also the perfect time to send mysterious messages.

Remember those disappearing ink letters? You write a message in lemon juice and it appears only when held to a candle or a high-watt lampbulb. Address the envelope in a flowing spidery hand—or something a bit weird and spooky. Write your note in lemon juice and add a penned note with the instructions to hold the notepaper to a lighted candle at the stroke of eight—or whatever hour you choose. The note can be one of those treasure hunt–types that instructs you to call a certain number that gives you a further clue, and so on. The "treasure" could be a Halloween party invitation, or a dinner invitation, or tickets to *The Phantom of the Opera!*

♥ THANKSGIVING DAY ♥

Thanksgiving is a time to be glad the one you love loves you!

Although Thanksgiving is generally considered a family celebration, and couples in relationships are subjected to the inevitable choosing of which family they will spend the holiday with, it is also a time to reaffirm how glad and grateful they are to have each other's love.

There are cards that emphasize these thoughts, but taking the time to sit together, to hold hands and tell each other how important this love is, will enrich the relationship immeasurably.

Another nice custom is to have each person at the Thanksgiving table share two things for which he or she is thankful. These unrehearsed "thanks from the heart" are love-bonding and greatly appreciated. Capturing these moments on video is a nice touch.

When couples are from different cultures, celebrating each other's customs is a lovely gift of caring.

Ruth, an American, was living on the island of Corfu in Greece while she wrote a novel. The man in her life, Dimitri, was a Greek soldier. As Thanksgiving approached, Ruth felt homesick, and mentioned to Dimitri that this was the first time she had been away from her family for Thanksgiving. He asked what the holiday was about, and, in halting Greek, she explained about the first Pilgrim's Thanksgiving. Several days later, Thanksgiving afternoon, Ruth was surprised by a knock at the door. Dimitri was supposed to be on duty. But there he was, dressed as much like an Indian as he could manage—topped off with a feathered headband!—and bearing a turkey his uncle had roasted in his bakery oven!

Ruth says that to this day she has never had such a wonderful Thanksgiving celebration—or such loving!

♥ SPECIAL CHRISTMAS CELEBRATIONS ♥

Christmas is traditionally a time for remembering, for showing how much we care and love the special people in our lives.

Perhaps of all the Christian holidays, Christmas is the one that epitomizes the caring, loving gesture, the physical and emotional statement of love. Because it is so highly charged with expectations, this season also carries the greatest potential for disappointment and disillusionment. To keep your holiday from ending in depression city, put the emphasis on caring and showing your love through those personal gestures that mean far more than fancy, expensive presents decked out in ribbons and bows.

The best present at any time of the year is one that involves the giver.

Fill a Christmas stocking or jewelry box with little decorated envelopes carrying minicertificates offering a massage with scented oils, a luxurious shampoo, sharing a candlelight dinner in a meadow, a stroll in the moonlight, a sleigh ride at a country inn—romantic gestures that require the gift giver to be involved. These "love gifts" can be claimed, one at a time, at any time during the year. Expect a lot of mistletoe kisses for your thoughtfulness!

Although there is a tendency toward buying practical things and appliances as Christmas gifts, try putting some of the season's magic into your selections.

The latest kitchen gadget or new workshop device may be on your love's want list, and, although highly desirable, these items are hardly the stuff of romance. Why not bring back your childhood custom of hanging up a stocking on the mantel or in a doorway, or setting out a shoe to be filled with surprises?

Darlene and Jim hang a big pair of ski socks on their bedpost each Christmas Eve. They have filled these with individually wrapped little fun gifts for each other: puzzles, miniature games, minibooks, tie clasps, costume jewelry, nuts, oranges, Swiss or Belgian chocolates—all wrapped and stuffed into the socks. On Christmas morning, they have a great time tearing through their socksful of treasures, sharing kisses and hugs and exclamations of delight!

♥ ROMANTIC CELEBRATIONS ♥
WITH FOOD

For a simple, fruit-based "love-bite," try this.

Peel a fresh, juicy ripe peach, cut it into sections, and soak it in a cup of chilled champagne. Finger feed it to your darling, bite by luscious bite. Dip a chilled washcloth into the residual champagne/peach juice and cool your sweetie's fevered brow and earlobes. Kiss/blow/nibble them dry. Peachy!

Even order-in food can have a romantic theme.

The special person in your life loves pizza—any time of the day or night. Take the opportunity to turn their craving into a romantic message by ordering a heart-shaped pizza and serving it on your best china, complete with candlelight and romantic music! None of your local shops has a heart-shaped pizza? Bake your own in a heart-shaped pan or cut a regular one into the desired shape. Try the same scenario using crêpes or french toast for a memorable "love you" breakfast!

Summer and early fall are the perfect seasons for a Western style barbecue for two.

Stack up your Dolly Parton, Kenny Rogers, and other Western singer favorites and get ready to party—Western style! Barbecue some ribs, hamburgers, or steaks, add flavorful ears of corn and baked potatoes or potato salad, and you have the fixin's for a down-home dinner. Serve beer, wine, or soft drinks from a galvanized tub—or a wheelbarrow—packed with ice.

A rustic table setting—colorful plastic is fun—brightened with a big bunch of field flowers, and lit with oil lanterns or Mexican tin lamps to cast a soft glow, sets the right tone.

Swirl about in a fringed, full-skirted outfit topped with a colorful neck scarf. Your partner is probably decked out in jeans and a plaid shirt, cowboy hat and boots—you might even have matching shirts and footwear!

A word of warning: slow-dancin' to those mellow, heart-throbbing Westerns will get you hungry for more than the barbecue!

Try this unusual arrangement when serving a plate of raw vegetables.

Give an hors d'oeuvres platter a boost by arranging the veggies to spell your love's name or initials—or form a big heart! Drizzle with a special creamy dill or curry sauce for added

pizazz. If you are feeling really artistic, you might try spelling
I LOVE YOU, TOM!

Surprise the one you love with a midnight snack—with a difference!

Heart-shaped waffles smothered with chocolate-dipped strawberries and whipped cream are a delightful *lover*ly snack to
put your darling in a "sweet" mood. If coffee doesn't keep
you awake—or if that is your intention—serve an exotic
blend, perhaps one flavored with a hint of cinnamon or chocolate or even Tia Maria, and topped with whipped cream.
You can both work off the calories trying out "new" positions
inspired by your "sweetness."

For centuries, pomegranates have been a popular "love fruit"

The bride in the beautiful *Song of Solomon* from the Old Tes-
tament promises, "I will give you mulled wine to drink and
fresh juice of the pomegranate." For hundreds of years, the
pomegranate, with its numerous seeds, has been associ-

ated with fertility and sexual potency throughout the Middle East and the Mediterranean.

Never let it be said you don't "care a fig" about being romantic!

The fig is not only symbolically sexual because of its testicular shape and its many tiny seeds (read *sperm*), but it is highly favored as a heightener of sensual pleasures. A bowl of fresh figs on the bedside table is an open invitation to a night of passion!

♥ BIRTHDAYS ♥

Add a special "zip" to the ordinary surprise element of a birthday celebration.

A birthday often marks an opportunity to surprise the celebrant with an unannounced party. This idea wears thin after a few times, and is not terribly inventive.

How about an intimate candlelit dinner in the privacy of your bedroom, attired in your birthday suits? He *could* wear a bow tie and she a necklace, but that is the limit permitted for "apparel!"

A hotel restaurant dinner "dessert" to remember forever!

Many couples celebrate birthdays or anniversaries by going to a ritzy hotel for dinner and/or dancing. This is lovely, but somewhat boring. To add a memorable touch to the evening, excuse yourself just prior to ordering dessert on the pretense of visiting the washroom or making a phone call. Having already arranged for a king-sized "playground" in one of the more elaborate rooms of the hotel, have the waiter deliver a note on a silver tray to your waiting loved one. The note announces that "dessert" is being served in your room immediately. A puzzled person arrives at the room to find *you* wearing a big bow—and perhaps little else—a dessert cart, and a steaming pot of french vanilla flavored coffee. Or you may have opted for a bottle of champagne! A sweetly unforgettable ending to a seemingly uneventful birthday dinner!

Is your darling a gambler at heart? Give your love his or her weight in poker chips. A lucky happy birthday!

Some people love to play cards—fun get-togethers where poker chips are used instead of money. Give your big-time gambler a real run for his or her money by contacting a poker chip wholesaler and buying enough to equal his or her weight. The chips are redeemable to "get lucky" with you. Raise the ante according to the heat generated: ten chips for a steamy kiss, fifty chips for a full-body hug, seventy-five chips for a full-body *naked* hug, one hundred chips for ??? Use your imagination. Expect *your* weight in poker chips on *your* next birthday!

♥ "JUST BECAUSE CELEBRATIONS" ♥

Bestow royalty on your favorite person: Buy a title!

If you have always fancied calling your dear one "My Lord" or "My Lady," then take the opportunity to make an anniversary royally special by purchasing an authentic title. Often there is an estate or castle attached. Pricey? Yes, but available—through either Sotheby's or Christie's auction houses in New York and London. They'll be happy to send you a list of titles currently on the market and the going prices. Next thing you know, you'll be wanting your morning papers ironed!

For an extravagantly romantic dinner, this one is near the top of the list!

Locate a hotel or restaurant complex where there is a glass-walled elevator with a view of the city. Arrange to rent this elevator for the evening of your grand celebration. What a beautiful setting for a romantic dinner for two, with the glittering lights of the city for a backdrop.

The Westin Hotel in Singapore offers a Valentine's Day package along these lines. You can choose the various floors where you want the elevator to stop: a different floor—and view—for each course, for example. With such a grand setting, one might even be inspired to propose!

*There's something inexpressibly romantic about a boat
and a clear expanse of water.*

Perhaps it's the feeling of being away from the rest of the
world for awhile, just the two of you. Whether you are in a
rowboat, a canoe, or a fabulous yacht, sharing a private world
surrounded by water—even for a few hours—is highly romantic. A rustic or elaborate picnic complete with champagne, wine, cider, or soft drinks, and perhaps some soft
music, adds to the sense of a romantic haven to be shared
with love. A good sunscreen and those mandatory lifejackets
are a further symbol of caring. Contrary to what you might
imagine, lifejackets have never been known to interfere with
the "course" set by true love!

*While you are enjoying the sun and sand, this beach
game will be "treasured" for a long time!*

Tell the lovely person you are on vacation with that there is
a treasure hidden in the beach sand at the resort where you
are staying, and that you found a "treasure map" with all the
details. But first your love must perform the "rite of love" in
order to obtain the map. . . . Now that you are both smiling,

hand over the map and a small shovel. When directions are followed, your sweetheart will "dig up" a pair of wine glasses or flutes protected by plastic wrap.

The next treasure spot hides a bottle of champagne packed in a bucket of ice to share as you watch the sunset from the beach. You could add a note to look in your shorts pocket. This last "treasure" might be either a ring, a necklace, a gold coin, a ticket, or a coupon for a night on the town, or instructions to kiss the "treasure"—you—depending on whether you are getting engaged or celebrating an anniversary, or just teasing. Fun and games time!

A "remember the fun" vacation lengthener.

While you are on vacation together, discreetly buy some extra postcards and address them to your darling. The cards will generally arrive a few days after your return. These make a neat way to remind your traveling companion of those romantic moments shared under the spell of a tropical moon— or wherever! Even if the vacation proved to be a disaster, the cards will give both of you something to laugh about!

♥ ANNIVERSARY ♥

A coupon box of unusual "presents" is sure to be warmly welcomed as an anniversary (or birthday) remembrance.

There are all kinds of little tasks that may not seem special, but when someone offers to do them for you they are greatly appreciated. Assemble a "coupon box" using a small file box and a dozen or two 3 × 5 cards. On each card, write a chore you are willing to do when your loved one needs it, with no questions asked. For example, you could offer a car wash, sewing on a missing button, cutting the grass, picking up dry cleaning, doing special laundry, running the vacuum sweeper, or doing the grocery shopping. Decorate each card with a little cartoon or heart for extra smileage!

An unusual way to celebrate an anniversary.

If you feel that your darling has made your life lighter and brighter, show your appreciation. Pack a picnic hamper and celebrate a sunset—or sunrise—from the basket of an air balloon sailing high over the countryside. Dazzlingly magical!

Innovative Ways to "Pop the Question"!

♥ ♥ ♥ ♥ ♥

A unique way to show you are ready to ask the "big question!"

Vince wanted Amanda to know that he was ready for the "big day" in a big way! He rented a luxurious white stretch limo and had it decorated with white wedding bows and ribbons. He dressed up in formal "morning wedding" attire—complete with gray gloves and spats. When Amanda opened the door and saw the limo and Vince's outfit, she couldn't believe he would go to such lengths to set the scene. Vince dropped to one knee and proposed, offering her a tiny white velvet box. Inside was a gorgeous solitaire. A blushing Amanda accepted, and the two of them dashed off in the limo to a celebratory lunch at a prominent downtown hotel. What flair!

A "novel" way to present that all-important ring!

Looking for a unique way to give your special love an engagement ring? Buy her the latest book from her favorite author. Lift the cover and cut out a space in the center pages big enough to fit the ring or ring-box into. Gift-wrap the book and casually present it. There will be nothing "casual" about her reaction!

Another "bookish" will you? twist.

Make a bookmark out of lightweight card paper and write the words, "Will you marry me?" on it and slip it into a book your love is currently reading. Better remember to sign your name!

Be daring and different when proposing to the love of your life.

Derek wanted an unusual setting for his proposal to Wanda. They were both flying to New York to a sociology conference, and Derek took this opportunity to "pop the question." He arranged with the flight crew ahead of time to have a bottle of champagne ready, and to have the captain announce his proposal. When the flight was well underway, the captain made the announcement, and the steward presented the blushing fiancée with the champagne—and a lovely gift of Passion perfume from the airline's onboard gift shop. Wanda enthusiastically accepted Derek's proposal, and the entire cabin cheered as they kissed. The happy couple was walking on cloud nine for days afterward!

Have your proposal "all wrapped up."

Ned was always doing something surprising. When he decided to present Babs with an engagement ring, he knew a truly unique approach was called for.

A friend of his sold large household appliances, so he obtained a huge cardboard box, had it beautifully wrapped and topped with a big red bow. The bottom of the box was left open so he could get into it. When Babs arrived home, the box was sitting on her front porch. What a surprise when she opened it and found Ned, dressed in a tuxedo, holding a bouquet of red roses and a white velvet ring box! Another friend of Ned's captured the whole scene on video for a lasting memento of the Big Moment!

This scenario offers a great way to present an engagement ring!

Imagine a chauffeured Rolls-Royce driving up to your front door to deliver a bouquet of white orchids and an invitation to join your darling in the smoked window interior. That was Ron's way of proposing to Debbi. They had been sweethearts for several years, but had not set a wedding date or even given it much thought until Debbi's closest friend asked her to be Maid of Honor and Debbi caught the bridal bouquet!

With visions of wedding veils and five-tiered cakes dancing in her eyes, Debbi let Ron know that she was open to suggestions. Ron's answer was the limousine and a gorgeous antique emerald and diamond ring, which he presented to her on the way to the courthouse to pick up their license!

Make use of childhood memories to create a memorable engagement moment.

Vanessa loved old-fashioned carousels. Her favorite animal was a beautifully decorated white horse that made the rounds in a nearby park. Brad arranged to reserve the carousel for a specific time on a lovely summer evening. When Brad and Vanessa arrived, he escorted her to her mount. Taking the adjoining horse, he held her hand as they circled to the music. A short time later, Brad moved from his steed and climbed up behind her and whispered his proposal. A surprised, ecstatic Vanessa said yes as Brad slipped a shining ring on her finger. Then Vanessa noticed that her whole family and Brad's were on the rest of the carousel animals! Everyone was smiling and clapping. Three hanky time!

A woman can also "pop the question"!

Shari loved wintertime. Her favorite sports were skiing and ice skating. When she and Ben had been dating for quite some time and seemed to be compatible, she decided to ask Ben to marry her instead of waiting for him to get around to it. After the first heavy snowfall of the season, she hired a horse-drawn carriage for a ride through the snow-covered countryside. While they jounced along, cuddled close under a blanket for warmth, she proposed. A surprised and delighted Ben answered, *"Yes!"* They returned home ringing the sleigh bells in celebration of the moment.

A top-of-the-world setting is perfect for the "big moment!"

Tamara wanted to ask Leon to marry her, but she didn't want anyone around in case he said no. So she asked the manager of the Ferris wheel concession at the fairgrounds where she and Leon were working to let the two of them go up alone after the fair closed for the night. He agreed, and said she could have five minutes at the top. She then told Leon she wanted to show him something special and it could only be seen from the top of the Ferris wheel. A puzzled Leon went along with her request, and when they were swinging high between earth and stars, Tamara popped the question. Leon hugged her close and whispered a "Yes" as *she* slipped a ring on *his* finger! The happy couple were still floating when they reached the ground.

Wedding Locations and Ceremonies

♥ ♥ ♥ ♥ ♥

Today's bride and groom have a wide choice of type of ceremony as well as location. Whether a couple is being married for the first time, or renewing their vows, there are many truly romantic things you can do. Many couples write their own vows incorporating favorite lines of poetry and quotations. Some ceremonies even mix various aspects of different religious faiths including Shinto or Buddhist chants. Most clergymen are willing to go along with these preferences as long as the basic pledge to each other is solemnized.

Today's brides often plan to include elements of ethnic ceremonies such as those indigenous to African, Indian or Far Eastern cultures. Recently, a bride who hailed from Ireland and was marrying a New Yorker, had Irish step dancers perform at her reception. Another had dances from an array of African tribes with the dancers in authentic dress.

One couple, who loved the music, dance and dress of the 1920's, requested that their guests also dress in 20's style. They referred to magazines from that period to choose wedding outfits and customs that were popular during that period. With the resurgence of the popularity of music in the 50's and 70's, these decades could also be a focus for the celebration. Why not a Victorian wedding theme? Formally lovely! With imagination and research, a couple can create a highly original ceremony that will give themselves and their guests pleasant memories.

Locations that are important to the couple themselves are, more often than not, upstaging local chapels. Sites as diverse as exotic islands, trains and cruise ships, underwater caverns, hilltops and alpine meadows, and prominent landmarks like the Eiffel Tower—all have served as the setting for exchanging vows.

Nostalgia figured prominently in one couple's ceremony. The guests were taken by chartered bus to celebrate the wedding at the place where the couple met as they retold the story of their first date. Fortunately, they hadn't met in Timbuktu!

Choose an unusual setting for your wedding and start your life together, or renew your vows, with a sense of being truly unique and special.

A wedding can take place virtually anywhere—even while skydiving! One daring couple in Sheffield, England, Laurie and Bentley, loved skydiving. They were able to locate a minister who also loved the sport. The three of them formed a "flying formation" while the couple exchanged their vows. Theirs was indeed a "happy landing!"

Like the song, "A Bicycle Built for Two," intrepid cycling couples have added this sport to their wedding ceremony.

Imagine a bride arriving at the chapel pedalling her multi-speed racing bike, her dress carefully tucked around her and her veil trailing in the breeze! Heidi's attendants arrived in the same way—all on bikes. The groom and best man had arrived on a tandem—a bicycle built for two—which the bride and groom used for the ride to the reception after the ceremony. Even the little flower girl rode her tricycle!

However, the happy couple accepted her uncle's offer of a limo for the ride to the airport for their flight to France. They planned a honeymoon cycling tour of Provence!

Some couples are really "up in the air" over their wedding plans!

Recently, in Arlington, Virginia, a young couple who are flying enthusiasts, rented a helicopter for the bride's arrival at the church. She alighted and greeted her attendants on the wide church lawn in time for the processional. After the ceremony, the elegantly dressed bride and groom circled the city where they had met, then buzzed off to a small local airport to join attendants and guests for a photography session on the tarmac followed by a beautifully catered reception in the huge airport hangar. The wedding cake decoration featured a miniature bride and groom in a tiny airplane and the caption, "Flight to Happiness!"

To make your ceremony really different, why not hold a sunrise wedding?

Maisie wanted all her close friends to be able to come to her wedding, but so many of them were working shifts and weekends that she finally settled on a 6:00 A.M. ceremony with a breakfast reception. She and Eddie exchanged their vows in the tiny church chapel just as the sun rose and filled the room with golden light. A memorable moment!

Consider this location for a "romantic high!"

Kevin and his bride, Arlene, headed for the eightieth floor of the Empire State Building in New York City for their "high on romance" wedding. To make the occasion doubly delightful, they chose February 14th as the date—as did thirty-one other couples! You might say their married life got started on a "high" note!

Endnote

♥ ♥ ♥ ♥ ♥

All of the tips and ideas in this book are designed to show that having fun as a couple is only limited by the borders of your creativity. Couple country is a fun place—enjoy its celebrations to the utmost!

In all of the tips in *Romancing the One You Love*, major emphasis has been placed on communication, on telling and showing the one you love how much you care—as often as possible! Even in difficult moments, a whispered "I love you so very much" can go a long way toward healing injured feelings.

One of the most important facets of a couple's life together, the sexual connection, is enhanced when a fun-loving, open attitude pervades these most intimate of all moments.

Keep smiling, kissing, hugging, laughing, and loving: *Your* relationship can only get better!

Marie Papillon has been hailed as *the* authority on love and romance. All over the world, men and women have learned her secrets of amour with fantastic results. Now, in her phenomenal bestselling book, she reveals:

• How, where and even when to meet that special someone—from walking the dog to working out to hosting a "blind date" party

• How to become an irresistible flirt—mastering verbal and non-verbal techniques...from making eye contact to talking on the phone to computer flirting!

• Tips for rekindling passion—from planning romantic menus for "theme evenings" to sending a bouquet of balloons and other creative ideas!

• Helpful hints for romance on a budget

• And much more!

A Million and One Love Strategies

Marie Papillon

A MILLION AND ONE LOVE STRATEGIES
Marie Papillon
_____ 95466-2 $5.99 U.S./$6.99 CAN.

- *Should women draw a line between love and sex?*
- *When are fantasies harmful—and when are they helpful?*
- *Is "sex addiction" truly a sickness?*

Bakos answers these and other questions with prescriptive advice that any woman can use to enjoy fulfilling sex and lasting relationships. In the author's singularly personal style, and in the words of hundreds of women from around the U.S., *Sexual Pleasures* brings wisdom, comfort, and sound counsel *to* women, *from* women.

SEXUAL PLEASURES
What Women Really Want,
What Women Really Need
SUSAN CRAIN BAKOS

SEXUAL PLEASURES
Susan Crain Bakos
_____ 92847-5 $4.99 U.S./$5.99 CAN.